RAFFIA EMBROIDERY

Dedication

For Mummy, Grandad and Nanny.

Thank you for your love, belief and support.

Acknowledgements

I'm so grateful for the opportunity to write this book. It has been a joyful, inspiring and, at times, challenging experience, but I've loved every part of it. I'm especially grateful to a few people whose support made this a reality.

Mummy, I couldn't have done this without you! Thank you for seeing and nurturing my creativity from the beginning. You've always believed in me (even when I didn't believe in myself), supported me through everything and encouraged me to keep going. With all my love, thank you for everything.

To my Grandad, Lazare Sylvestre (1939–2021), thank you for always being there for me. From the school runs to sharing stories of your St Lucia with me. Your love and support meant so much, I feel so lucky to have had a grandad like you. I miss you every day and I promise to keep making you proud.

To my Nanny, Holifay Sylvestre, thank you for being there from day one. I'm so grateful for your love, encouragement and care. Thank you for being a safe place for me, for your endless support and sharing your Jamaica with me.

To my close family, thank you for your love and for always being there to support when it mattered most.

To Miss Winterton (aka Sarah), my textiles teacher, thank you for recognizing my creativity and always encouraging me to pursue it. You always went above and beyond as a teacher. Your belief in me and continued support mean everything.

To Carrie and the lovely Search Press team, thank you for this amazing opportunity. I'm so grateful for your guidance and all the hard work you've put into this project.

To the Caribbean, the nature, culture and craft of the region continue to inspire me, and I've loved getting to learn more through my creative practice.

And finally, to the Windrush Generation, thank you. Your strength and resilience have paved the way for so many of us. I carry your legacy with pride and gratitude.

TIHARA SMITH

RAFFIA EMBROIDERY

VIBRANT DESIGNS INSPIRED BY THE CARIBBEAN

CONTENTS

INTRODUCTION

I was first introduced to raffia embroidery while creating my graduate fashion collection, inspired by my Caribbean heritage and the stories of the Windrush Generation. I knew I wanted to base my collection on my heritage – something I've always been proud of, often hearing stories of 'back home' from my grandparents while growing up. My fashion collection became a personal exploration of my Caribbean background, from my grandparents' experiences to the wider stories of the Windrush Generation who journeyed to the UK from the 1940s to the 1970s.

My grandparents are part of the Windrush Generation. My Grandad arrived in London from St Lucia as a teenager in 1958; my Nanny made a similar journey from Jamaica a few years later. They met in London and built their family and a new life together. Their stories, captured in their memories and family photographs, became the basis of my research, alongside interviews with family and studying photography from the time.

One element that particularly interested me was the straw craft souvenirs that often decorated the 'front rooms' of the Windrush Generation. These objects represented both a connection to their Caribbean roots and a distinctive way of personalizing their new London spaces. This sparked an idea: could I reinterpret these traditional techniques in a contemporary way that combined my Caribbean heritage with my London perspective?

A research trip to a London fabric store introduced me to natural raffia fabric, which reminded me of the traditional Caribbean woven straw work I admired. After initial embroidery experiments with paper and synthetic raffia, I landed on the raffia embroidery technique you'll learn in this book!

My final graduate collection became a blend of my experience as a Londoner with my Caribbean heritage. Now, I'm excited to share the enjoyment of raffia embroidery with you, so you too can create stunning pieces that tell your own stories.

WINDRUSH

The term 'Windrush Generation' refers to the Caribbean people who migrated to Britain between 1948 and 1973. Named after one of the first ships that arrived in Britain in 1948, the *Empire Windrush* carried hundreds of passengers from places like Jamaica and Trinidad.

After the Second World War, Britain faced widespread damage and labour shortages across various sectors such as construction, transportation and healthcare. By 1948, the Nationality Act was passed which gave people from British colonies, including parts of the Caribbean, the right to live and work in Britain. People from the Caribbean travelled to Britain in search of work and new opportunities; many would have been attracted by official recruitment drives by British government bodies.

Almost 200 passengers arriving in the UK on board the Empire Windrush in 1948 cited crafts like dressmaker, hatter, tailor, shoemaker, upholsterer and artist as their profession. Many of the Windrush Generation also practised craft skills such as crochet, knitting, embroidery and smocking, which played a significant role in the decoration of the Caribbean 'front room'.

Below, left: my Nanny, Holifay, stylishly dressed, in her mid–late twenties (circa 1970s/1980s).

Middle: my Grandad, Lazare, looking sharp in his trilby hat; he always had a taste for Italian tailoring. He bought this 'slim Jim' tie from a door-to-door salesman who would come at weekends to sell clothes and accessories (circa 1960s).

Right: my Nanny's parents, Joseph and Merlina, with friends at a London wedding. I didn't get to know my great-grandad Joseph, but I have nice memories of great-grandma Merlina, a talented seamstress. I like to believe I inherited some of my creative talents from her!

The Windrush Generation has played an important role in British society by contributing to various fields such as art, music, sports, politics and healthcare. Their contributions have paved the way for future generations of Black British Caribbeans who have continued to make a significant positive impact to British society.

As members of the Windrush Generation, my grandparents' stories, memories and photographs greatly inspire my creative practice. Through this book, I am delighted to honour the legacy of the Windrush Generation and my grandparents, while building upon the creativity of Caribbean crafts and sharing a piece of Caribbean culture with you.

The contributions of the Windrush Generation are honoured and celebrated annually in the UK on Windrush Day, 22 June.

Left: My grandad with his friend Vernon in Dulwich, South London. The cap is the first cap he bought when he came to London.

Above: My Grandad with one of his best friends, Martin, outside their home at the time in Aldgate East, London (circa 1960s/1970s).

CARIBBEAN STRAW CRAFTS

The raffia embroidery in this book takes inspiration from traditional Caribbean straw craft. While much of Caribbean culture, including its crafts, hasn't been extensively documented, here's a glimpse into what I've learnt.

Early traditions and indigenous influence

The story of Caribbean crafts is intertwined with the region's history. Though the indigenous population sadly declined due to European colonization, those who survived are believed to have passed down their knowledge of agriculture and crafting, including straw work. These early Caribbean craftspeople were masters of using local materials to create functional items for everyday life. Their skill and resourcefulness live on through the traditional crafts that have been passed down for generations, keeping a vital part of their culture alive.

A blend of cultures

The arrival of enslaved Africans and indentured labourers from various countries, like India and China, further enriched Caribbean culture. Their diverse skills and knowledge blended with existing practices, resulting in a distinctive blend of styles and techniques reflected in local crafts.

Left: me, outside the Castries Central Market, St Lucia. Here you can find a variety of local crafts, souvenirs and fresh produce. I'm wearing a dress designed and made by a local maker (taken in 2019).

Below: my grandad (on the right) performing with his steel pan band (circa 1960s/1970s).

Far left: a beautiful view of Castries, St Lucia, from Howelton Estate, known for its arts and crafts experiences on the island (photo taken on my 2019 holiday).

Left: a view of the Pitons in St Lucia. This photo was taken by my Grandad on a trip back to St Lucia (circa 1980s).

From plant to product

Caribbean craftspeople are masters at transforming readily available plant materials like sisal, vetiver grass (also known as khus khus grass) and screw pine into beautiful and functional objects. The process begins with the careful selection of raw materials – strong, yet flexible blades of grass or leaves. These natural fibres are then meticulously cleaned, dried and skilfully woven, plaited or sewn into a wide variety of items, from hats and baskets to mats, chairs and even bags. Each piece, whether a woven basket designed to carry heavy produce, or a straw hat decorated with floral embroidery, tells a story of the craftsperson's resourcefulness, creativity and deep appreciation for the natural world.

A tradition in transition

Sadly, straw crafts are a dying art in many areas of the Caribbean. While the tradition continues, particularly in rural areas, it struggles to captivate younger generations. As younger generations are drawn to more modern interests, the knowledge and skills that have been passed down for centuries are at risk of being lost.

My exploration of Caribbean straw crafts and raffia embroidery was, in part, a way to pay tribute to the skills and knowledge passed down through generations in the Caribbean. It's a chance to appreciate the beauty and functionality of straw crafts while creating a modern take on this longstanding tradition. Although raffia itself as a material isn't as widely used in the Caribbean as other materials like sisal, the creativity and resourcefulness that defines Caribbean straw crafts is what truly inspired me to explore this technique using a straw material that was available to me. Like the Caribbean craftspeople before me, I was inspired to use the 'straw' readily available to me in London – raffia fabric!

WORKING WITH RAFFIA

I've spent a lot of time studying straw bags and fans – souvenirs from my own holidays to St Lucia and gifts, like the examples shown below, brought back by family from their visits 'back home' to St Lucia and Jamaica. I also studied images of other beautifully crafted straw hats, bags and fans, focusing on the decorative stitches used by the craftspeople who made them. This exploration helped me to recreate these effects in my own way, ultimately leading to the simple yet effective technique you'll learn in this book!

The beauty of the raffia embroidery used in this book lies in its simplicity. All you need is paper and synthetic raffia ribbon, stitched onto a base of natural raffia fabric. This combination unlocks creative possibilities, allowing you to craft stunning patterns, words and tropical motifs in a vibrant colour palette.

Texture also plays a crucial role in bringing your designs to life. The natural raffia's matte finish creates a beautiful contrast with the smooth paper and the sheen of synthetic raffia, adding depth and dimension to your designs. However, if you prefer a more natural look, natural and paper raffia come in a wide range of colours, allowing you to create stunning artwork without plastic.

Much like other crafts, raffia embroidery is great for practising mindfulness as it has a relaxing, repetitive nature to it. As you stitch, you'll find yourself unwinding and de-stressing, leaving your worries behind with each stitch.

I hope this book will be your ultimate starter guide for raffia embroidery, welcoming both beginners and experienced stitchers.

Three outfits from my graduate collection, shown at Graduate Fashion Week in 2018.

TOOLS AND MATERIALS

Each project has its own list of supplies, but here we look at the tools and materials that will be used throughout all the projects.

RAFFIA RIBBON

Raffia ribbon is used as the embroidery thread in raffia embroidery. It comes in a variety of colours, and you can choose from natural raffia, paper raffia and synthetic raffia.

1. Paper raffia ribbon

The main raffia ribbon used in this book is paper raffia ribbon. There is a rainbow of vibrant colours to choose from, and it is supplied in continuous lengths with a uniform appearance, making it the perfect embroidery thread with raffia fabric.

2. Synthetic raffia ribbon

Synthetic raffia can make a great embroidery thread as, like paper raffia, it has a continuous appearance, is reasonably strong and durable and is available in a range of colours.

The combination of synthetic raffia alongside paper raffia for embroidery on a base of natural raffia creates a beautiful textural contrast, as synthetic raffia adds a touch of shine against the matte finish of natural and paper raffia.

To minimize the use of plastics, synthetic raffia ribbon is used sparingly in the projects in this book. However, you can still achieve wonderful results using only paper raffia, if you wish to avoid using plastics in your crafts.

3. Natural raffia ribbon

Natural raffia ribbon is made from the leaves of the raffia palm or the palmyra palm tree. The leaves are stripped and dried, then sorted by length, width and colour. Raffia is typically sold in hanks or skeins and by weight.

Natural raffia comes in its natural colour, a light tan or straw colour, or it can be dyed. Due to the natural colour variations in the fibres, dyed raffia may not appear perfectly even. Unlike typical embroidery thread, natural raffia is not one continuous strand but instead consists of individual strands up to around 1.5m (1.6yd) long, limited by the length of the leaf it came from. The width of the raffia strands can also vary.

In this book, I don't use natural raffia ribbon due to the inconsistency of the strands' width and the more limited colour palette.

3
2
1

RAFFIA FABRIC

Natural raffia fabric is used as the base for raffia embroidery. It is made from natural raffia strips tied together, then woven to create a loose weave fabric. Typically sold by the metre, but also as a sheet, it is often used for making hats and bags. It is a somewhat sculptural and stiff fabric that boasts a textural quality. There are two types of raffia fabric: coarse weave and narrow weave.

You can find raffia fabric in specialist fabric shops or millinery supplies shops. If you can't find raffia fabric, hessian makes a good substitute, as it has a similar loose weave that allows your needle and raffia ribbon to glide through the fabric.

As raffia fabric is made from natural fibres, it may have slight imperfections such as joining knots or inconsistencies in the weave. However, this is normal and adds to the unique character of your embroidered piece.

Raffia is a wipe-clean-only fabric.

TIP

When working with raffia fabric, there isn't a 'right side' – you can simply choose which side you'd prefer to stitch on!

Left: (1) natural raffia fabric with a coarse weave; (2) natural raffia fabric in a finer weave, which has been treated to change the colour; and (3) hessian fabric.

OTHER MATERIALS

1. Embroidery thread/floss

Six-strand cotton thread is used in some projects for finishing.

2. Felt

Felt fabric is used to finish the back of embroidery hoop projects.

3. Cotton fabric

Plain cotton fabric is used in some projects for lining or finishing.

4. Fusible interfacing

While not always necessary, interfacing can be helpful in raffia embroidery. Fusing interfacing to the back of the raffia fabric helps stabilize it before embroidering. Woven raffia fabric can fray at the edges, so interfacing also helps prevent fraying along the cut edges of your raffia fabric.

Choosing the right interfacing allows you to maintain some flexibility in the raffia fabric, or help keep it stiff, depending on the project. There are two main options to consider: stretch or woven.

Stretch interfacing helps maintain some flexibility, while still offering stability. Despite raffia not being stretchy itself, a soft, lightweight stretch interfacing can be a good choice.

Woven interfacing is another option, particularly for projects that don't require flexibility. This offers a firmer base for embroidery.

Both types of interfacing come in fusible varieties, so they can be bonded to the back of the raffia fabric using heat. Always follow the manufacturer's instructions, which will detail the ideal temperature and application time for fusing, and it's crucial to test your chosen interfacing on a scrap piece of raffia fabric before applying it to your entire project.

TOOLS

1. Quilting hoops

A hoop keeps the raffia fabric taut, preventing bunching or warping, and is more comfortable on your hands. While any depth of hoop can be used, deep quilting hoops are ideal for raffia fabric. Choose a hoop that comfortably fits your design, allowing enough extra fabric around the edges. If your design is too large for the hoop you have, you can move the hoop around as you work.

2. Scissors

You will need fabric scissors to cut and trim the raffia fabric and any other fabrics. Use sharp embroidery scissors for cutting raffia ribbon and thread. Use paper scissors to cut paper raffia ribbon and the project templates (avoid using your fabric scissors for paper as it will blunt them).

3. Needles

The large eye of a chenille needle accommodates the wide raffia strands: size 18 is good for raffia embroidery. Chenille needles have a sharp point which allows the needle to pierce through the raffia fabric easily. Regular sewing needles are fine when using embroidery thread/floss.

4. Tracing wheel and carbon paper

Use a tracing wheel to transfer the embroidery templates to raffia fabric. It works with dressmakers' carbon paper (see page 23). Carbon paper comes in different colours; dark colours work well with raffia fabric.

5. Permanent marker

Use a fine-tip permanent marker to darken the transfer lines on raffia fabric. Use either a colour close to the natural raffia fabric base or the raffia ribbon you are using. I like to use a Sharpie ultra fine point permanent marker in brown.

6. Clear-drying fabric glue or PVA glue and glue brush

Apply a clear-drying fabric glue to the seams of raffia fabric to prevent fraying. PVA glue can be used to secure ends of raffia ribbon. Use a small (clean!) paint brush to apply glue to the fabric.

7. Screwdriver

It's handy to have a flat head screwdriver to help loosen and tighten the screw on quilting hoops.

8. Sewing machine thread

I recommend a good quality all-purpose thread such as Gütermann Sew All Thread. Colour 414 is a good match with natural raffia fabric.

9. Pins and clips

Dressmaking pins and fabric clips are handy when sewing projects together or to pin templates to fabric.

10. Fastenings

You will also need zips, bag straps, snap fasteners and twine for finishing your projects.

11. Sewing machine

A sewing machine (not pictured) is used for most projects to prevent the raffia fabric from fraying and for the construction of the finished projects after embroidery. It can also be useful to have an overlocker (or serger) to create neat seams, but this is optional as you can use the zigzag stitch on a regular sewing machine as an alternative.

12. Iron or heat press

An iron (not pictured) is necessary to fuse interfacing to raffia fabric, smooth out hoop marks after removing your project from the quilting hoop, and to press seams. A heat press (see page 21) is an optional tool but can be used for fusing interfacing to raffia fabric.

9
7
Essentials
WHITECROFT
DRESSMAKERS
TRACING PAPER
PAPIER À TRACER
KOPIERPAPIER
for all your haberdashery needs
8
100% Polyester
12
6
THE CRAFT PLACE
Fabric Glue
150ml
2
4
6mm
12 Sets
Snap Fasteners
Rust-Proof Brass
Hemline
10
10
3
1
9
Sharpie
5

TECHNIQUES

This section includes all the techniques you need to know to start and finish your raffia embroidery projects.

PREPARING THE RAFFIA FABRIC

Raffia fabric has a lovely, loose weave, but this makes it prone to fraying. To help minimize this, and to add some stability to your raffia fabric, I recommend fusing a lightweight stretch interfacing to the wrong side of the fabric. Remember to test a small piece of raffia fabric with your chosen interfacing before proceeding with your project.

1 Cut the necessary amount of raffia fabric.

2 Cut a piece of interfacing slightly smaller than the raffia fabric. This will prevent the interfacing from hanging over the edge and the adhesive from sticking to your ironing surface.

3 Place the right side of the raffia, which you will embroider onto, face down on your ironing board. I recommend using an old ironing board cover or protecting your ironing surface with a scrap piece of fabric, as adhesive from the interfacing can sometimes transfer onto it.

4 Position the interfacing on the wrong side of the raffia fabric, with the rough adhesive side down. To protect both your iron and the raffia fabric, place a piece of scrap fabric over the interfacing.

5 Following the manufacturer's instructions, use an iron or heat press to fuse the interfacing to the raffia fabric.

TIP

Experiment with different types of interfacing to achieve various effects. A stretch interfacing, commonly used for knit fabrics, can help maintain the flexibility of the raffia while providing stability. A stiffer interfacing can be used for projects that require more structure.

I like using a heat press, shown on the left, rather than an iron when fusing interfacing, as it provides consistent heat and pressure. This is especially useful for larger pieces. It can also help create a better adhesive bond between the interfacing and the fabric, and its larger plate helps save time.

TRANSFERRING THE EMBROIDERY TEMPLATES TO RAFFIA FABRIC

Each project has a template in the back of the book (see pages 110–127), printed at actual size.

To use the templates, either photocopy the template you wish you use, or trace it onto plain paper, then follow the steps below to transfer the design onto your raffia fabric.

Note that using a tracing wheel to transfer the design to fabric can create small indents on the paper, in which case you may need to take a fresh photocopy or tracing if you wish to reuse a transfer.

TIP

It is advisable to use a craft mat or cutting mat underneath your raffia fabric to protect your work surface when using the tracing wheel.

1 Cut around the template.

2 Place your prepared raffia fabric on a flat surface.

3 Position the template on the fabric where you want the embroidery to be with a sheet of carbon paper beneath it, with the coloured side facing the fabric (I recommend red or blue carbon paper).

4 Secure it in place on the raffia with one or two pins.

5 Use a tracing wheel to trace the lines of the template onto the fabric. The carbon paper will transfer the design with dotted lines.

6 Remove the pins, carbon paper and template from the fabric. You should now have a dotted outline of the design on the raffia fabric.

7 To make the outlines easier to see, use a fine-tipped permanent marker (brown or a colour similar to your raffia ribbon) to draw over the lines ready for embroidery.

PLACING THE RAFFIA FABRIC IN THE HOOP

Quilting hoops are deeper than standard embroidery hoops, making them better suited to thicker raffia fabric. If possible, choose a quilting hoop large enough to fit your entire embroidery design. If you don't have one big enough, you can move a smaller hoop around as you work.

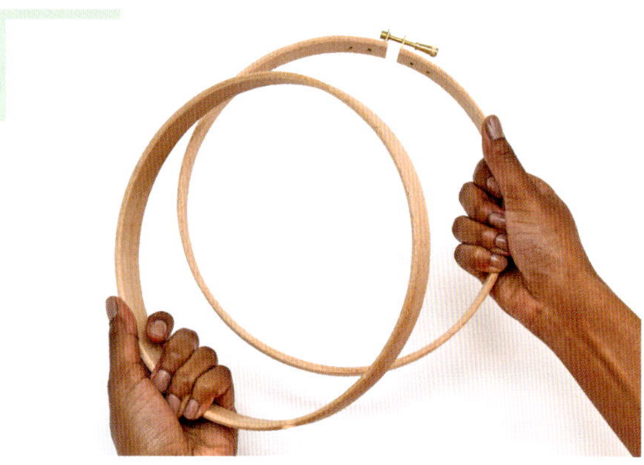

1 Loosen the screw on the hoop and separate the inner and outer parts, then place the inner hoop (without the screw) on a flat surface.

2 Centre your prepared raffia fabric over the inner hoop, ensuring it's positioned as desired for your embroidery project.

3 Take the outer hoop (with the screw) and carefully place it over the fabric and inner hoop.

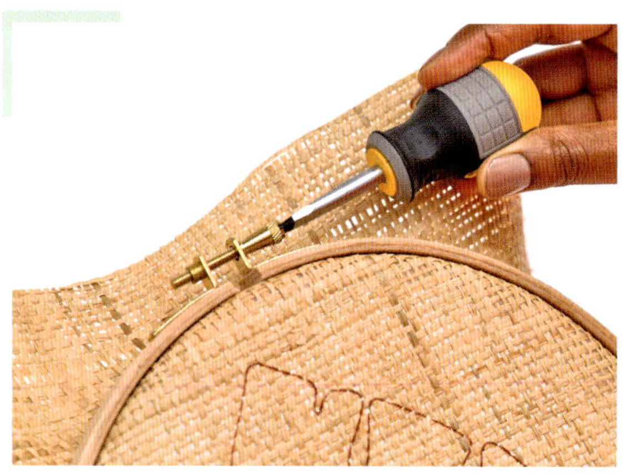

4 Gently press down on the outer hoop to secure the fabric in place.

5 Tighten the screw to firmly hold the fabric in the hoop.

6 If necessary, gently pull the edges of the fabric to ensure it's taut, but avoid excessive pulling, as this can cause fraying.

THREADING THE NEEDLE WITH RAFFIA RIBBON

One of the benefits of raffia embroidery is how easy it is to thread the needle with raffia ribbon. I recommend using a size 18 chenille needle as its large eye perfectly accommodates raffia ribbon.

1 Cut a length of raffia ribbon in your desired colour. Cut about an arm's length to prevent tangling. To create a fuller, more textured stitch, unfold the raffia ribbon to its full width. Leave approximately 3cm (1¼in) of one end folded.

2 Use the folded end of the raffia ribbon to guide it through the eye of the chenille needle.

3 Leave about a 10cm (4in) tail. There's no need to tie a knot at the end of the ribbon.

SECURING THE RAFFIA RIBBON

There's no need to tie a knot at the end of raffia ribbon when threading the needle (see page 25), as you can secure your first stitch with a double knot at the back. This helps reduce bulk on the back of projects.

1 Create your first stitch (see pages 28–37 for embroidery stitches), leaving a 10–15cm (4–6in) tail at the back. Turn the hoop to the back/wrong side.

2 Take the tail you left and your working piece of ribbon and cross one over the other.

3 Tie one knot.

4 Tie a second knot to double knot and secure the stitch. Trim the excess ribbon from the tail. You can now continue stitching.

FINISHING THE WRONG SIDE OF EMBROIDERY WITH GLUE

Some projects need the reverse side of the embroidery to be as flat as possible to reduce bulk when assembling the project. One way to do this is to use PVA glue to stick down the tails at the back of the embroidery instead of knots. For these projects you would not secure the raffia ribbon on your first stitch as shown opposite.

1 Turn your finished embroidery to the wrong side and trim the tails to 1–2cm (½–¾in) in length.

2 Using a glue brush, apply PVA glue to the trimmed tail.

3 Stick the glued raffia tail down onto the back of the raffia fabric using your finger. If it doesn't stick at first, add a bit more glue and apply more pressure.

4 Repeat for all loose tails.

TIP

Leave the PVA glue to dry according to its packaging instructions, or for at least an hour.

EMBROIDERY STITCHES

Several embroidery stitches work well with raffia embroidery. Different types of stitches create different textures and looks for your designs. As raffia ribbon is quite a thick embroidery thread, simple, bold stitches tend to work best. Before starting projects, I recommend testing stitches on a small piece of raffia to familiarize yourself with the stitch and establish a stitching rhythm.

STRAIGHT STITCH

A straight stitch is a fundamental stitch in embroidery, forming the basis for many other stitches. It involves a simple, single stitch that can be horizontal, vertical or diagonal. By varying the length of these stitches, you can create a wide range of patterns and designs in your embroidery.

1 Bring the needle up through the fabric to the right side. Leave a short tail of raffia (about 10cm/4in) on the back.

2 Take the needle back down to the back of the fabric at the desired stitch length.

3 Pull the raffia all the way through to create one stitch. Tie together the short tail you left at the beginning with the longer working end of the raffia (see page 26). This secures your work.

4 Continue stitching as desired.

BACK STITCH

Back stitch is a good outline stitch and can also be used on its own to create a bold line.

1 Start by creating one straight stitch.

2 Bring the needle up a stitch length beyond the first stitch, as shown on the left.

3 Bring the needle back down through the hole of the previous stitch, as shown on the left.

4 Repeat steps 2 and 3 for all remaining stitches.

RAFFIA FILL STITCH

Raffia fill stitch, similar to a satin stitch in traditional embroidery, is useful for covering large areas with dense, straight stitches, creating a beautiful and textured fill. As you work raffia fill stitch, keep the tension on the raffia ribbon consistent to avoid tightness or looseness in your embroidery.

1 Start by bringing your needle up to the front of your fabric, just outside the edge of your design. Leave a short tail of raffia (about 10cm/4in) on the reverse.

2 Take your needle down, just outside the design line as shown, to create your first straight stitch.

3 Bring the needle up again, close to the first stitch and still outside the design line, and back down again so the stitches sit alongside one another.

4 Before continuing, turn the embroidery hoop to the wrong side. Here, tie together the short tail you left at the beginning with the longer working end of the raffia to secure your work.

5 Now, return the hoop to the front. Continue stitching in rows across the entire shape you want to fill. Keep your stitches close together for smooth and full coverage.

BLANKET STITCH

Blanket stitch is a great stitch for finishing and decorating edges.

1 Bring the needle through your fabric, or brim of the hat in this instance, leaving a 10cm (4in) tail on the wrong side.

2 Bring the needle over the edge and back up through the same hole to create a loop.

3 Thread the needle through the loop from right to left, as shown above. Pull to secure.

4 Bring the needle up to create a loop. Thread the needle through the loop from right to left. Pull to create the first stitch.

5 Repeat step 4 for the remaining stitches.

6 Tie a knot through the previous stitch to finish.

CHAIN STITCH

Chain stitch creates a series of looped stitches that form a chain-like pattern.

1 Bring the needle up through the fabric, leaving a short tail of raffia ribbon (about 10cm/4in) on the wrong side.

2 Bring the needle back down, right next to or through the same hole, to create a loop, as shown.

3 Bring the needle up, ensuring the needle is coming up through the loop. Pull the raffia to create your first chain stitch.

4 Repeat these steps for the remaining stitches.

5 To end a row of chain stitches, make a tiny stitch over the last loop, securing the stitch in place.

Finishing the back of chain stitch

Finishing a row of chain stitch is different than the method shown on page 24. In this case, we secure the first stitch at the end.

1 Turn your work to the back and thread the needle through the last stitch and tie a knot to finish. Trim the excess raffia ribbon.

2 Go back to the first stitch where you left the short tail, thread the tail through the needle and thread the needle through a stitch at the back.

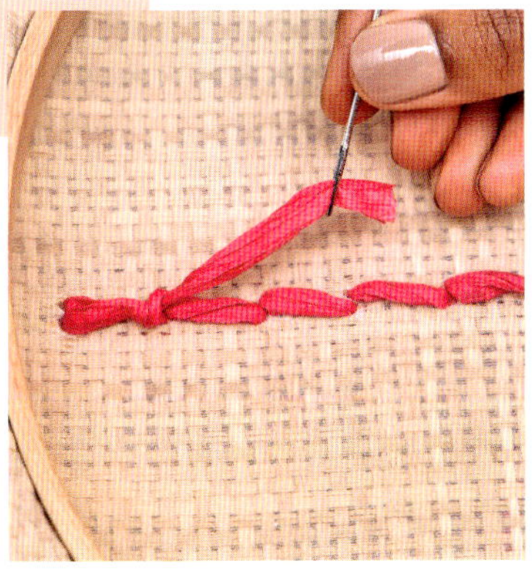

3 Tie a knot to finish.

THREADED BACK STITCH

Threaded back stitch is a decorative stitch using a foundation of back stitch and a second thread woven under the stitches to create a wavy effect.

1 Create a line of back stitch (see page 29) with your first length of raffia ribbon/colour.

2 Bring the second raffia ribbon/colour up through the same hole as the first backstitch.

3 Slide the needle under the next backstitch, then pass it back under the following stitch. Continue weaving the raffia from one side to the other.

4 Take the thread down at the final stitch and secure at the back with a knot.

STEM STITCH

Stem stitch is a lovely decorative stitch with a rope-like appearance and is also great for outlining.

1 Create one straight stitch (page 28), then bring the needle up midway along the first stitch.

2 Bring the needle back down to create a straight stitch the same length as the first.

3 Repeat to create a line of stem stitch.

FERN STITCH

Fern stitch is a beautiful decorative stitch utilizing straight stitch in different directions to create a pattern.

1 Bring the needle up and down again to create a straight stitch (see page 28). Secure the raffia ribbon at the back as shown on page 26.

2 Bring the needle up through the fabric about 1cm (½in) *above* the end of your first straight stitch. Insert the needle in the same hole as the beginning of your first stitch to create a diagonal stitch.

3 Bring the needle up through the fabric about 1cm (½in) *below* the end of your first straight stitch.

4 Insert the needle in the same hole as the beginning of your first stitch to create another diagonal stitch.

5 Bring the needle up one stitch length away from the end of your first straight stitch, and then back down into the same hole as the end of your first straight stitch to create a back stitch (see page 29).

6 Repeat steps 2–5 to continue your fern stitch.

Difficulty ratings

When you begin the projects in the next section, you will see that each project has a difficulty rating, indicated by the number of leaf icons as follows:

THE PROJECTS

MONSTERA LEAF HOOP ART

This is a simple and stylish project to get you started with raffia embroidery. Use the basic fill stitch to create a textured monstera leaf in your favourite shade of green. Hang your finished piece to add a touch of the tropics to your living space.

FINISHED SIZE

- 20 x 20cm (7¾ x 7¾in), when presented in a hoop

MATERIALS

- 30 x 30cm (12 x 12in) piece of raffia fabric
- 30 x 30cm (12 x 12in) piece of fusible stretch interfacing
- Embroidery thread (any colour)
- 30 x 30cm (12 x 12in) piece of felt fabric
- Template from page 111

RAFFIA RIBBON COLOURS

- Green

EQUIPMENT

- 20cm (7¾in) quilting hoop
- Carbon paper
- Toothed tracing wheel
- Fine-tip permanent marker, brown
- Chenille needle
- Fabric scissors
- Paper scissors

Prepare the raffia

1 Prepare the raffia using the method in the techniques section (see page 20).

2 Set your sewing machine to the longest stitch length. Sew around the perimeter of the prepared raffia fabric to prevent fraying.

Transfer the embroidery template

3 Transfer the monstera leaf design to the centre of the prepared raffia fabric using the technique on pages 22–23.

4 Place the raffia fabric in the quilting hoop (see page 24).

Embroidery

5 Thread the chenille needle with an arm's length of raffia fabric (see page 25).

6 Fill the monstera leaf embroidery design using raffia fill stitch (see page 30).

Finishing the back of your hoop

8

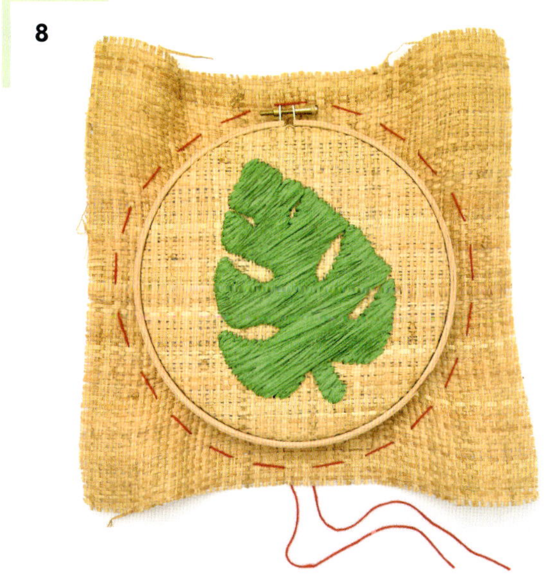

9

10

7 Cut a piece of cotton embroidery thread three times the circumference of the hoop and thread it through a chenille needle – do not tie a knot at the end of the thread.

8 Sew a line of running stitch through the raffia around the circumference of the hoop, about 2–3cm (¾–1¼in) from the hoop edge, leaving a tail at the beginning and end of your stitches on the wrong side (the red thread in the photo).

9 Cut around your stitching, about 2cm (¾in) away, using fabric scissors, to remove excess fabric.

10 Pull on the embroidery thread tails to gather the raffia fabric to the back of the hoop. Tie a knot to hold the gathering together.

Sewing the felt backing to the hoop

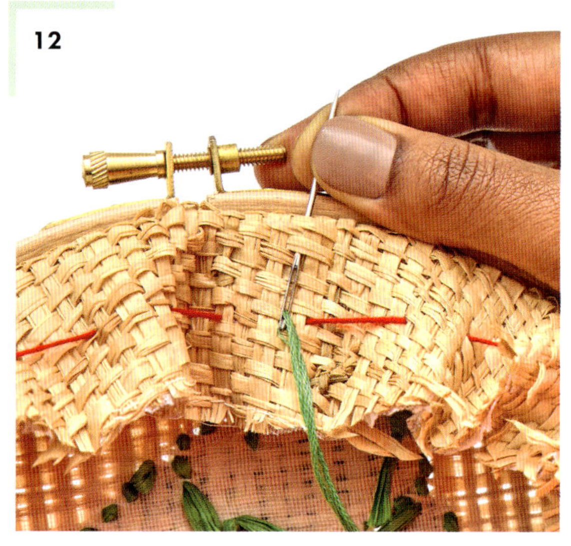
12

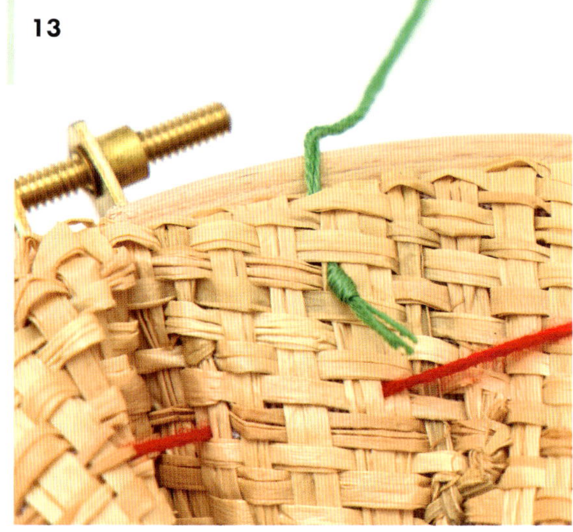
13

14

11 Cut an arm's length of embroidery thread and thread it onto your needle. Tie a double or triple knot at the end of the thread.

12 Sew through the raffia, over the inner hoop, as shown.

13 Pull through the knot.

14 Cut a circle of felt, using the hoop as a guide, and lay the felt circle over the back of the hoop.

15

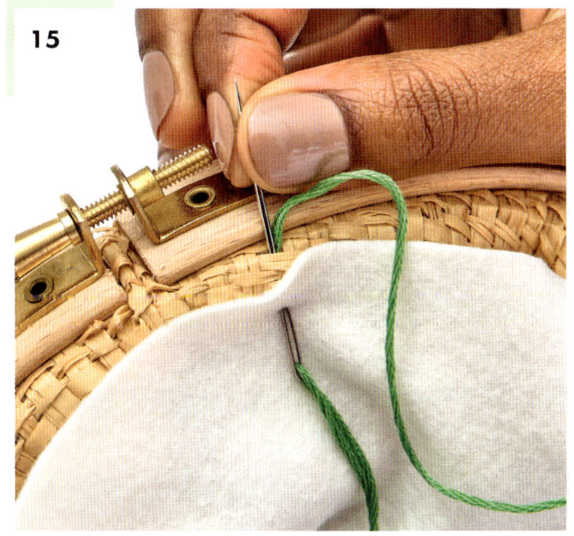

18

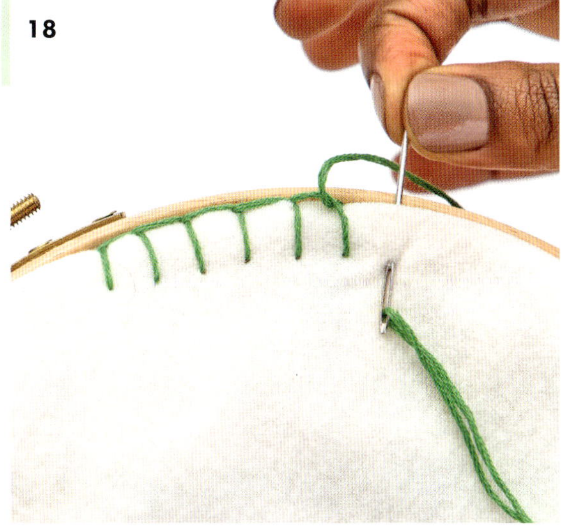

19

15 Sew through the felt and raffia, and over the inner hoop then pull through the thread.

16 Sew through the felt and raffia, again about 1cm (½in) away from the first stitch.

17 Pull through the loop, making sure the thread is over the loop.

18 Pull through the stitch. Continue stitching around the whole hoop.

19 When you've stitched around the whole hoop, tie a knot through the first stitch to secure. Then pull the needle through under the felt and cut the thread.

STRAW HAT

Elevate your summer style with this fun raffia embroidery straw hat. This project is all about making a hat distinctive to you! Choose your favourite raffia colours and embroidery stitches to create a unique, personalized design.

FINISHED SIZE

- Depends on your hat; mine measures 43cm (17in) in diameter, and the crown is 8cm (3in) deep.

MATERIALS

- Plain straw or raffia hat with a loose weave

RAFFIA RIBBON COLOURS

- Paper and/or synthetic raffia ribbon in a variety of colours

EQUIPMENT

- Chenille needle
- Paper scissors
- Measuring tape

Visitors in the Folly, Not Counting the Coach House
rule, I had to carry the bloody thing from the trades-
man's entrance down into my lab all by myself. Molly

Plan your design

1 First, gather your straw hat and your chosen raffia ribbon colours.

2 Refer to pages 28–37 and choose up to five embroidery stitches (in addition to blanket stitch) from the following:

- Straight stitch (page 28)
- Back stitch (page 29)
- Chain stitch (page 32)
- Threaded back stitch (page 34)
- Fern stitch (page 36)

3 Now it's time to get creative with your stitches! Decide on the order in which you would like your stitches and raffia colours. The number of stitches you choose will depend on the size and shape of your hat. Creating some quick sketches with coloured pencils or pens can be useful here, as I've done on the right.

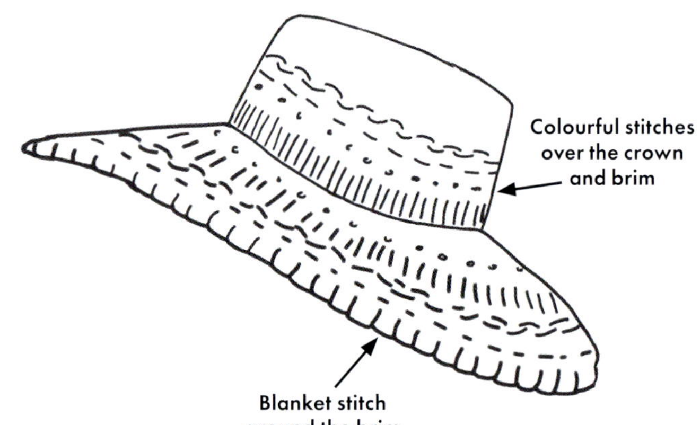

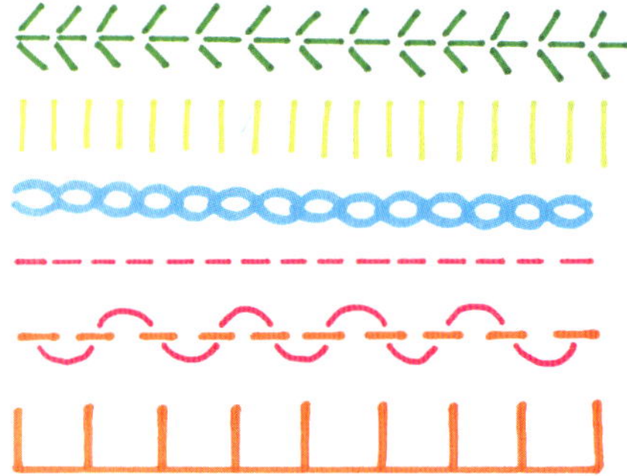

TIPS

Choose a hat with a loose weave to make sure you can easily pass your needle through with raffia.

This project can be made without the use of an embroidery hoop. However, if you find it easier to use an embroidery hoop, choose a small hoop that can fit the width of the brim of the hat and move it around as you stitch.

When you get to the hat crown, I would advise not using an embroidery hoop as it's too awkward to get it in place.

Remember, the inside of the hat matters too! As you work, take a quick look at the wrong side to ensure the raffia is fully pulled through each stitch and the underside appears neat, since you'll see this side too while wearing your hat.

Blanket stitch the brim

4 Start by adding a clean finish to the brim of your hat with the blanket stitch. Follow the instructions for the blanket stitch on page 31.

5 To ensure the distance between each stitch is consistent around the brim of your hat, use a measuring tape as you stitch.

Add more stitches to the brim

6 Decide on the gap that you want between each colour/type of stitch. I recommend 1–1.5cm (approx ½in).

7 Following the order of stitches you created earlier, begin your next row of stitches using your chosen gap measurement from the hat brim edge. Use a measuring tape as you stitch to keep the stitches consistent.

8 As you continue adding stitches, keep measuring the distance from the hat edge using a measuring tape to ensure consistent spacing.

Stitch the crown

9 Once you reach the base of the crown, it's time for a new stitch! This part of the hat can be a bit tricky, so I suggest using simple stitches like back stitch (page 29), straight stitch (page 28) and chain stitch (page 32).

10 Here, we'll switch our measuring reference point. Instead of measuring from the brim's edge, start measuring from the base of the crown to ensure consistent stitches around the crown.

11 Continue adding rows of stitches upwards, always measuring from the crown's base to keep your stitches even.

12 Keep stitching until you reach the top of the hat, or until you've covered the desired area.

PARROT WALL HANGING

Bring a piece of the tropics into your home with this vibrant raffia embroidered parrot wall hanging. Inspired by the souvenirs of the Windrush Generation, this project uses basic fill stitches and the unique texture of raffia to create a stunning decorative piece.

FINISHED SIZE

- 40 x 36cm (15¾ x 14in), including fringe

MATERIALS

- 60 x 60cm (23¼ x 23¼in) piece of raffia fabric
- 60 x 60cm (23¼ x 23¼in) piece of fusible stretch interfacing
- 40 x 40cm (15¾ x 15¾in) cotton drill or canvas fabric
- 15mm (½in) thick wooden dowel, approc 47cm (18½in) long
- Twine
- Templates from pages 112–113

RAFFIA RIBBON COLOURS

- Black, brown, green, light green, turquoise, white, yellow

EQUIPMENT

- 30cm (12in) quilting hoop
- Carbon paper
- Toothed tracing wheel
- Fine-tip permanent marker, brown
- Chenille needle
- Fabric scissors
- Paper scissors
- Embroidery scissors
- Sewing machine
- Dressmakers' pins
- Iron
- Overlocker (optional)
- Pinking shears (optional)

Prepare the raffia

1 Prepare the raffia fabric using the method on page 20.

Transfer the wall hanging template

2 Using the diagram below, measure and draw the wall hanging outline on to paper. Cut this out, then pin it to your prepared raffia and draw around the outer rectangle shape with the fine-tip marker pen. Remember to mark the 8cm (3¼in) measurements from each corner on both the top and bottom lines with a small line (these correspond to the black triangles on the template).

3 Set your sewing machine to the longest stitch length. Sew a line around the entire perimeter of the paper template. Make sure the stitches stay within the drawn line. This sewn line will prevent the raffia from fraying when you cut it out later.

4 Now, switch your sewing machine to a stitch length of 3.5. Using this setting, sew two straight vertical lines from the top edge of your rectangle down to the bottom, following the marks you made for the black triangles on the template. These stitched lines will hold the raffia strands in place for the fringe you'll create later.

5 Take your wall hanging template and carefully position it within the central rectangle (the 24 x 30cm/9½ x 12in space) on the raffia. Secure it with a pin to keep it in place.

6 Transfer the design to the raffia fabric using carbon paper and a tracing wheel. Refer to page 22 for instructions on how to do this.

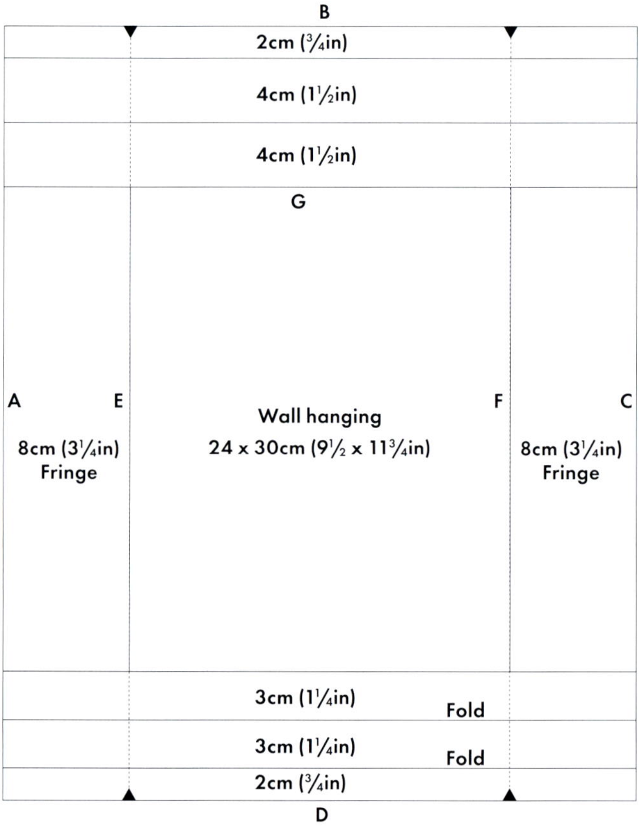

B
2cm (¾in)
4cm (1½in)
4cm (1½in)
G
A
E
F
C
8cm (3¼in) Fringe
Wall hanging 24 x 30cm (9½ x 11¾in)
8cm (3¼in) Fringe
3cm (1¼in) Fold
3cm (1¼in) Fold
2cm (¾in)
D

Embroidery

7 Place your raffia with the transferred design in the quilting hoop. Try to fit as much of the design in the hoop as possible, but don't worry, you can move the hoop around as you work.

8 Fill in the shapes of the design with a raffia fill stitch (see page 30) following the colours and arrows in the illustration below.

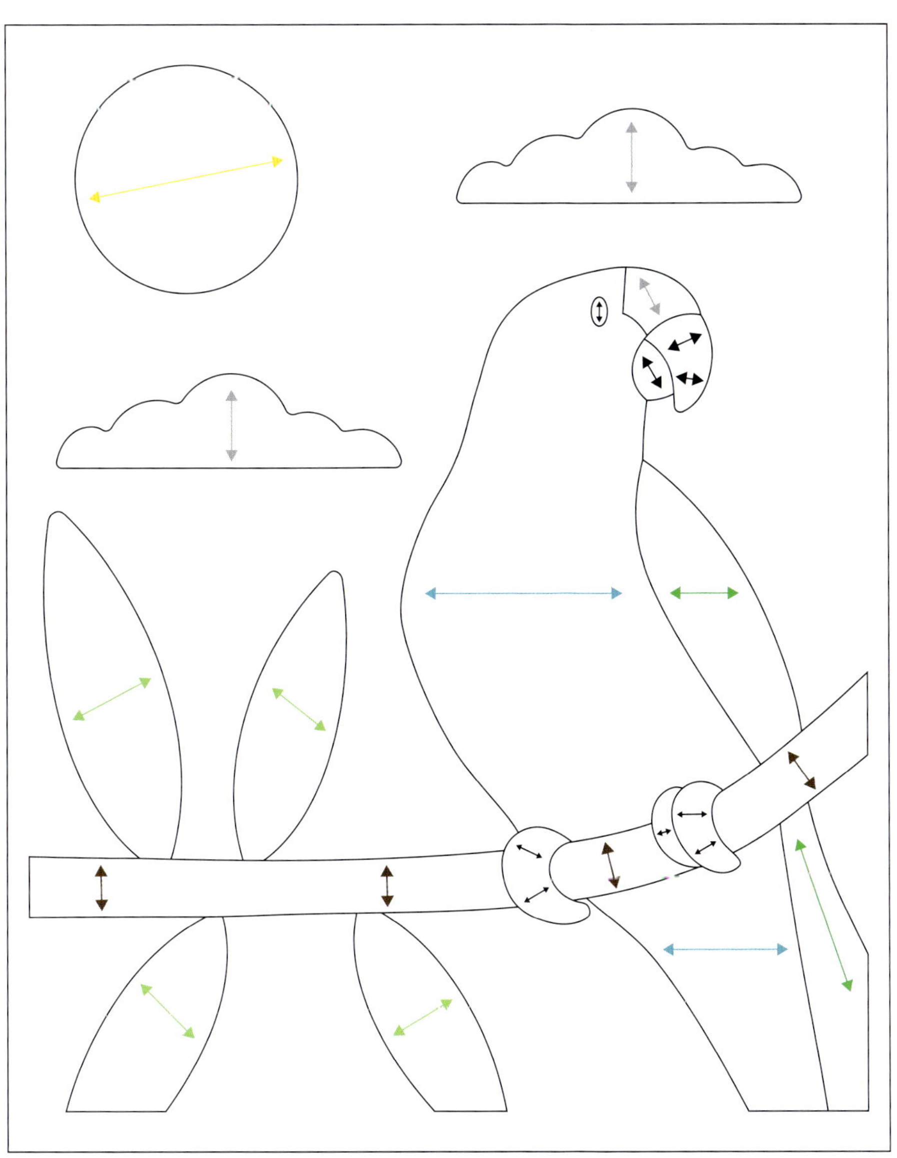

Prepare the lining (optional)

For a professional touch to your wall hanging, consider adding a lining to the back of the piece. Here's how to prepare it:

9 Cut the lining from your chosen cotton drill or canvas fabric using the measurements on the lining illustration below.

10 Neaten the raw edges labelled H, I and J in the diagram below, using your preferred method. Good options include:

- **a** Cutting the raw edge with pinking shears.
- **b** Sewing a zigzag stitch along the raw edges with your sewing machine.
- **c** Overlocking the raw edge with an overlocker machine.

11 To hem the edges, fold and press the designated fold lines on the lining fabric using an iron. Fold sides H and I by 1cm (¼in) and fold side J by 2cm (¾in). Hold the folds in place using dressmakers' pins.

12 Following the creases, sew straight lines down these folds with your sewing machine to create hems along edges H, I and J. This will create a polished finish.

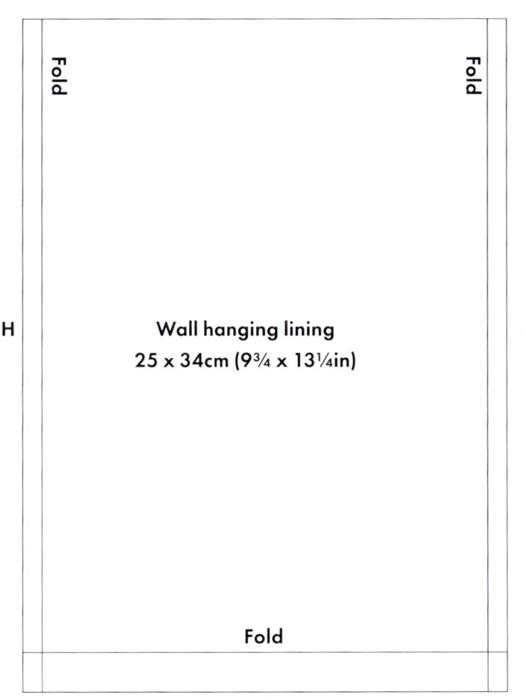

Assemble your wall hanging

Now that your embroidery is complete, let's transform it into a beautiful wall hanging! Follow these steps carefully, also referring to the template on page 54:

13 Using fabric scissors, carefully cut out the raffia wall hanging, staying just outside the stitching line to avoid cutting through stitches.

14 Focus on the vertical sides of the template labelled A and C. Here, snip away the stitches that hold these sides closed.

15 Next, comes the fun part – creating the fringe! Locate the fusible stretch interfacing between sections A–E and F–C. Peel it away carefully, stopping at the stitch lines at lines E and F. Don't remove any interfacing beyond the stitching.

16 With embroidery scissors (for extra precision!), trim off the peeled-away interfacing. Be super cautious not to snip through your stitching lines, as this holds the fringe and prevents further fraying.

17 Gently pull on a single vertical strand of raffia between points A and E, where you just removed the interfacing. This will start the unravelling process. Keep pulling out vertical raffia strands until you reach the stitch line at point E. Repeat this process on the other side (F–C).

Hem the wall hanging

18 Time to create a clean finish! Use your iron to fold and press the labelled fold lines along the top and bottom of the wall hanging.

19 If you opted for a lining, tuck the prepared lining under the top hem and secure it with pins. Leave the bottom hem of the lining untucked.

Sew the hems and hanging

20 Now that everything is in place, use your sewing machine to stitch along the folded edges of the top and bottom hems. This will create a neat and finished look.

21 Thread your wooden dowel through the gap in the top hem. To create a way to hang your masterpiece, tie a piece of twine or string securely to each end of the dowel.

BANANA DECORATION

Add a touch of tropical fun to your home with this adorable raffia banana hanging decoration. Use raffia fill stitch to create the banana shape, and back stitch to create the decoration. Hang it anywhere for a cheerful and playful accent to your space.

FINISHED SIZE

- 5cm x 22cm (2 x 8½in)

MATERIALS

- 40 x 40cm (15¾ x 15¾in) piece of raffia fabric
- 40 x 40cm (15¾ x 15¾in) piece of fusible stretch interfacing
- 40 x 40cm (15¾ x 15¾in) piece of felt fabric (1mm)
- Embroidery thread (I used DMC 738)
- Fabric glue or PVA glue
- Template from page 111

RAFFIA RIBBON COLOURS

- Brown, yellow

EQUIPMENT

- 30cm (12in) quilting hoop
- Carbon paper
- Toothed tracing wheel
- Fine-tip permanent marker, brown
- Chenille needle
- Fabric scissors
- Paper scissors
- Embroidery scissors
- Dressmakers' pins

Prepare the raffia

1 Prepare the raffia using the method on page 20.

Transfer the banana template

2 Place the banana embroidery template on your prepared raffia fabric. Secure it with a pin to keep it in place.

3 Transfer the design to the raffia using carbon paper and a tracing wheel. Refer to page 22 for detailed instructions on how to do this.

Embroidery

4 Place the raffia with the transferred design in your quilting hoop, ensuring the entire design fits in the hoop – in this project you won't be able to move the hoop around while you embroider.

5 Using the raffia fill stitch (see page 30), fill in the banana shape following the colours and arrows in the illustration shown.

Note: do not knot your raffia at the beginning or end of stitches. Leave the ends loose on the back of your work.

Finish the back of your embroidery

6 Remove your completed raffia embroidery from the quilting hoop.

7 Turn your work over to the back. Trim the loose raffia ribbon ends to prevent them from hanging over the edge when folded.

8 Use fabric glue or PVA to secure these ends to the back of the raffia design, as shown on page 27. Allow the glue to dry completely.

9 Place the felt fabric on a flat surface, then position your embroidered raffia on top, with the design facing upwards. Secure this sandwich in your embroidery hoop.

Assemble your raffia embroidery banana decoration

10 Cut a length of embroidery thread about an arm's length long. Thread it onto your needle without knotting the end.

11 Leave about 10cm (¼in) of thread loose at the start. Using backstitch (see page 29), stitch around the entire embroidered fruit design. As you are stitching, keep looking at the back of your work to ensure your stitches are neat on the felt side.

12 Once you've completed the stitching, tie off the loose thread by passing it through a previous stitch and tying a knot.

13 Return to the beginning of your stitching where you left the loose thread. Thread it through the needle and tie it off with another stitch.

14 Remove your work from the embroidery hoop.

15 Using fabric scissors, carefully cut around your stitches, leaving at least a 5mm (¼in) gap between the cut line and the embroidery thread stitches. Be sure not to cut through the stitches. If preferred, use small embroidery scissors.

16 Cut a length of embroidery thread to your desired hanging length. Thread it into the needle without knotting the end.

17 Pierce the needle in and out through the felt backing where you want the decoration to hang.

18 Tie the ends of the hanging thread together in a knot or bow.

DON'T
WORRY
ABOUT A
THING

PILLOW COVER

Bring the tropics indoors with this uplifting raffia embroidery cushion cover. Use the basic raffia embroidery fill stitch to create a relaxing 'Take it Easy' design decorated with tropical leaves.

FINISHED SIZE

- 50 x 50cm (19½ x 19½in)

MATERIALS

- 55 x 55cm (21¼ x 21¼in) piece of raffia fabric
- 55 x 55cm (21¼ x 21¼in) piece of fusible stretch interfacing
- 80 x 60cm (31¼ x 23¼in) piece of cotton drill or canvas fabric
- Sewing machine thread in cream
- 50 x 50cm (19¼ x 19¼in) pillow pad
- Templates from pages 112–119

RAFFIA RIBBON COLOURS

- Variety of greens, orange

EQUIPMENT

- 45cm quilting hoop
- Carbon paper
- Toothed tracing wheel
- Fine-tip permanent marker, brown
- Chenille needle
- Fabric scissors
- Paper scissors
- Dressmakers' pins
- Sewing clips
- Iron
- Sewing machine
- Overlocker (optional)

TAKE IT
EASY

Prepare the raffia

1 Prepare the raffia fabric using the method on page 20.

Transfer the cushion cover template

2 Measure a 52 x 52cm (20½ x 20½in) square in the centre of your piece of raffia fabric and draw the outline of the square onto the fabric using the fine-tip marker pen and ruler. This includes a 1cm (¾in) seam allowance on all sides.

3 Set your sewing machine to the longest stitch length. Sew a line around the entire perimeter the square you just marked. Make sure the stitches stay within the drawn line. This sewn line will prevent the raffia from fraying when you cut it out later.

4 Take the cushion cover templates from pages 114–119 and carefully position them within the square marked on the raffia fabric, using the image below as a guide. Keep the templates at least 3cm in from the edges to allow enough space for the seam allowance. Secure the pieces with pins to keep them in place.

5 Transfer the templates to the raffia using carbon paper and a tracing wheel. Refer to pages 22–23 for instructions on how to do this.

Embroidery

6 Place your raffia with the transferred design in an embroidery hoop. As this is a large design, you will need to work section by section, moving the embroidery hoop as needed.

7 Fill in the shapes of the design with raffia fill stitch (page 30) and back stitch (page 29) following the colours, labels and arrows in the illustration shown.

Prepare your cushion cover front (raffia)

8 Your finished embroidery may have indentations from the hoop. You can smooth these out with an iron. To do this, place a piece of scrap fabric or an old bed sheet over your embroidery to protect it. Gently press the embroidery with a warm iron over the protective layer.

Important: avoid ironing directly on synthetic raffia as it will melt.

9 Using fabric scissors, carefully cut around the stitched square cushion cover shape, staying just outside the stitching line.

10 To prevent fraying, finish the edges of the raffia square. If you have an overlocker, use this to stitch around the raw edges. Otherwise, use a zigzag stitch on your sewing machine.

Prepare your cushion cover back (cotton)

11 Cut out two identical pieces, each measuring 52 x 36cm (20½ x 14in) for the back of your cushion cover, using your chosen cotton fabric.

12 Finish the raw edges of both fabric pieces. Overlock or zigzag stitch along one long edge and both short edges of each piece.

13 Create a hem on the remaining long edge of both pieces. Fold and press the edge over by 1.5cm (½in), then fold it over and press again by another 1.5cm (½in).

14 Sew this folded edge down with a straight stitch using your sewing machine.

Assemble your cushion cover

15 Place your completed raffia embroidery front piece right side up on a flat surface. Position one of the cushion cover back pieces face down on top, aligning the overlocked/zigzag stitched edges at the top and sides. Pin the layers together.

16 Create the envelope closure by placing the second cushion cover back piece face down on top of the first layer, aligning the overlocked/zigzag stitched edges opposite the first piece at the bottom. Secure the layers together with sewing clips or dressmakers' pins.

17 Using a sewing machine, stitch around the entire perimeter of the cushion cover, maintaining a 1cm (½in) seam allowance. When you've finished sewing, press open the seams using your fingers. This will help when turning the cushion right side out.

18 Carefully turn the cushion cover right side out, pushing out the corners to create a neat shape.

19 For an even neater finish, you can lightly press the edges of the cushion cover with an iron, using a protective cloth.

20 Place the cushion insert inside the completed cushion cover.

HIBISCUS ZIPPED POUCH

Accessorize your favourite summer looks with this beautiful hibiscus zip pouch. Embroider two vibrant flowers using fill and stem stitches, and then transform it into a stylish accessory.

FINISHED SIZE

- 30 x 21cm (12 x 8¼in)

MATERIALS

- 40 x 50cm (15¾ x 20¾in) piece of raffia fabric
- 40 x 50cm (15¾ x 20¾in) piece of fusible stretch interfacing
- 40 x 50cm (15¾ x 20¾in) piece of cotton fabric for lining
- Zip, 30cm (12in) long (I used YKK 001 yellow gold)
- Sewing machine thread in cream and yellow
- Clear-drying glue
- Templates from pages 120–121

RAFFIA RIBBON COLOURS

- Orange, pink, yellow

EQUIPMENT

- 30cm (12in) quilting hoop
- Carbon paper
- Toothed tracing wheel
- Fine-tip permanent marker, brown
- Chenille needle
- Sewing needle
- Fabric scissors
- Paper scissors
- Dressmakers' pins
- Fabric clips
- Sewing machine
- Iron
- Glue brush

Prepare the raffia

1 Prepare the raffia fabric using the method on page 20.

Transfer the hibiscus template

2 Measure two 32.5 x 22.5cm (12¾ x 22¾in) rectangles on your piece of prepared raffia fabric and draw the outline onto the fabric using a fine-tip marker pen and ruler. Each rectangle includes a 1cm (⅜in) seam allowance on all sides. Keep a gap of at least a 15cm (6in) between each rectangle. Mark the centre of each side with a small mark on both rectangles.

3 Set your sewing machine to the longest stitch length. Sew a line around the entire perimeter of the rectangle shapes you just marked. Make sure the stitches stay within the drawn line. This sewn line will prevent the raffia from fraying when you cut it out later.

4 Take the hibiscus templates from pages 120–121 and carefully position them within one of the rectangles on the raffia. Keep the templates at least 2cm in from the edges to allow enough space for the seam allowance. Secure with pins to keep the templates in place.

5 Transfer the templates to the raffia using carbon paper and a tracing wheel. See page 22 for detailed instructions on how to do this.

Embroidery

6 Place your raffia with the transferred design in the embroidery hoop. Try to fit the whole design in the hoop otherwise, you can work section by section, moving the embroidery hoop as needed.

7 Fill in the hibiscus petals with a raffia fill stitch (see page 30) following the colours and arrows in the illustration below.

8 Fill the hibiscus stamen with a line or two of stem stitch (see page 35).

TIP

You can choose to include the hibiscus design on one side of your pouch or both.

If you want to embroider on both sides, transfer the hibiscus design onto both rectangles of prepared raffia fabric in steps 5–6.

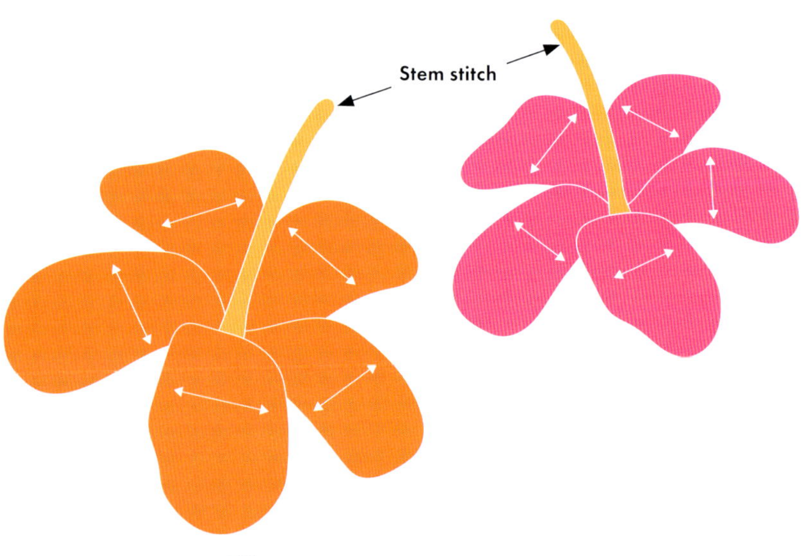

Cut out the raffia pieces and lining

9 Your finished embroidery may have indentations from the hoop. You can smooth these out with an iron. To do this, place a piece of scrap fabric or an old bed sheet over your embroidery to protect it. Gently press the embroidery with a warm iron over the protective layer.

Important: avoid ironing directly on synthetic raffia as it will melt.

10 Using fabric scissors, carefully cut around the rectangle shapes you marked onto the raffia, staying just outside the stitching line. You should have two rectangle pieces that will be the front and back of your pouch.

11 Fold your cotton fabric for the lining in half, following the grainline. Measure and draw a 32.5 x 22.5 cm (12¾ x 22¾in) rectangle on one side. Pin through both layers to hold them together, then cut out the rectangle with fabric scissors. Mark the centre of each side on both pieces. You should now have two rectangles for the pouch lining, including the seam allowance.

Prepare the zip

12 Fold the four ends of the zip tape, pin in place then tack down with a few hand-sewn stitches, as shown on the right.

13 Fold the zip in half and mark the centre on both sides of the zip teeth.

Sew the zip to the raffia and lining fabric

14 Lay the raffia front piece on a flat surface. Place the zip right side down at the top, matching the centre marks. Ensure the zip pull is on the left side when closed.

15 Secure the zip in place using fabric clips or dressmaker's pins.

16 Stitch the zip to the raffia with a 5mm (¼in) seam allowance. Begin sewing with the zip open and close it just before the end to avoid sewing near the pull.

17 Place the lining fabric right side down over the zip, aligning the centre marks. Secure with clips or pins.

18 Sew the lining to the zip with a 5mm (¼in) seam allowance over the first stitch using the same open-and-close technique as before.

19 Lightly press the lining away from the seam line. The seam allowance should be pressed towards the lining.

20 Sew an under-stitch by inserting your needle in the lining fabric close to the seam line. Use the ridge on the presser foot as a guide for straight stitching.

21 Fold the raffia and lining together with the wrong sides together, then finger press the seam. Then use an iron to neatly press the lining and raffia down, protecting the raffia with a cloth.

22 Top stitch on the raffia, 5mm (¼in) away from the seam.

23 Repeat steps 15–23 on the other side of the zip to create the back side of the pouch.

12a

12b

16

Assemble your pouch

24 Open the zip halfway.

25 Place the raffia pieces right sides together, and the lining right sides together.

26 Pin or clip around the pouch pieces, leaving a 20cm (7¾in) gap at the bottom of the lining.

27 Sew around the zip pouch pieces with a 1cm (½in) seam allowance, leaving a 20cm (7¾in) gap at the bottom of the lining unsewn. (Optional: before sewing, consider tacking the raffia together at the zip seam with some hand stitching to prevent shifting during machine stitching.)

28 Turn the zip pouch right side out, using a blunt object to push out the corners.

29 Press the raffia side of the pouch flat with a cloth, and press the lining side neatly, closing the lining opening.

30 Sew the bottom of the lining closed.

31 Push the lining inside the raffia pouch and close the zip.

Finish the seams (optional)

32 To prevent fraying and enhance durability, carefully apply a thin layer of clear-drying glue into the seams around the raffia pouch with a small paintbrush.

33 Allow the glue to dry completely for 24 hours.

TOTE BAG

Bring the beach with you wherever you go with this stylish raffia tote bag. Learn how to create a fun palm tree design using the fill stitch and transform natural raffia fabric into a summer essential.

FINISHED SIZE

- 45 x 33 x 14cm (7¾ x 13 x 5½in)

MATERIALS

- 70 x 120cm (27¼ x 47¼in) piece of raffia fabric
- 70 x 120cm (27¼ x 47¼in) fusible stretch interfacing
- 65 x 15cm (25¼ x 6in) piece of fusible woven interfacing
- 70 x 90cm (27¼ x 35¼in) piece of cotton fabric for lining
- Sewing machine thread in cream
- Pair of bag straps (I used 3mm (⅛in) wide Prym strapping webbing in yellow)
- Fabric glue
- Templates from pages 122–123

RAFFIA RIBBON COLOURS

- Brown, dark green, light green

EQUIPMENT

- 30cm (12in) quilting hoop
- Carbon paper
- Toothed tracing wheel
- Fine-tip permanent marker, brown
- Chenille needle
- Fabric scissors
- Paper scissors
- Dressmakers' pins
- Sewing clips
- Sewing machine
- Iron
- Glue brush

Prepare the raffia

1 Prepare the raffia fabric using the method in the techniques section (page 20).

Transfer the palm tree template

2 Measure and draw a 62.5 x 7cm (24½ x 2¾in) rectangle onto the raffia fabric. This gives you the facing piece, including a 1.5cm (½in) seam allowance.

3 Next, draw the shape of the tote bag outline, as shown in the diagram below. Keep at least a 2cm (¾in) gap between the bag pieces and the facing. Measure and draw each side carefully with a ruler and fine-tip marker pen. The shape include a 1.5cm (½in) seam allowance to all sides.

4 Repeat steps 2–3 so you have two tote bag shape outlines and two facing shapes drawn on your raffia fabric.

5 Set your sewing machine to the longest stitch length. Sew a line around the entire perimeter of each of the shapes you just marked. Make sure the stitches stay within the drawn line. This sewn line will prevent the raffia from fraying when you cut it out later.

6 Take your tote bag palm tree templates from pages 122–123 and carefully position them within one of the tote bag template shapes. Keep the templates at least 3.5cm (1¼in) from the edges to allow enough space for the seam allowance.

7 Transfer the templates using carbon paper and a tracing wheel. Refer to page 22 for detailed instructions on how to do this.

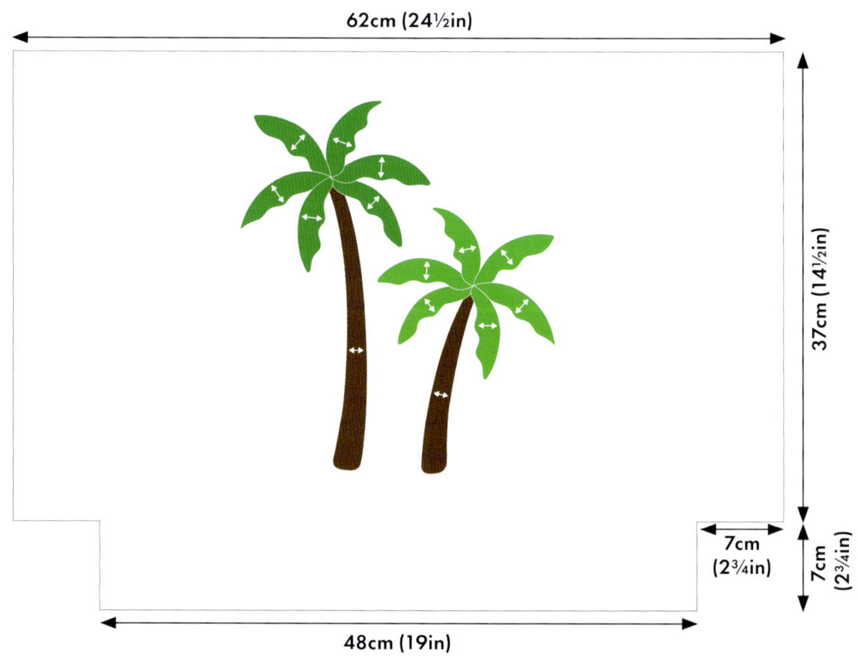

Embroidery

8 Place your raffia with the transferred design in the embroidery hoop. If the whole design doesn't fit in the hoop, you can work section by section, moving the embroidery hoop as needed.

9 Fill in the shapes of the design with a raffia fill stitch (see page 30) following the colours and arrows in the illustration to the right. Once finished stitching, remove the hoop.

Cut out the lining

10 Prepare your lining fabric by ironing it to smooth wrinkles. Fold the fabric in half, aligning the selvedge edges.

11 Measure and cut out two lining pieces, using the measurements in the diagram below.

12 Measure and cut out two 62 x 4.5cm (24½ x 1¾in) rectangles of fusible woven interfacing for the lining.

13 Iron one lining interfacing piece to the top edge of one of the lining pieces on the wrong side, following the manufacturer's instructions. Repeat on the other lining piece.

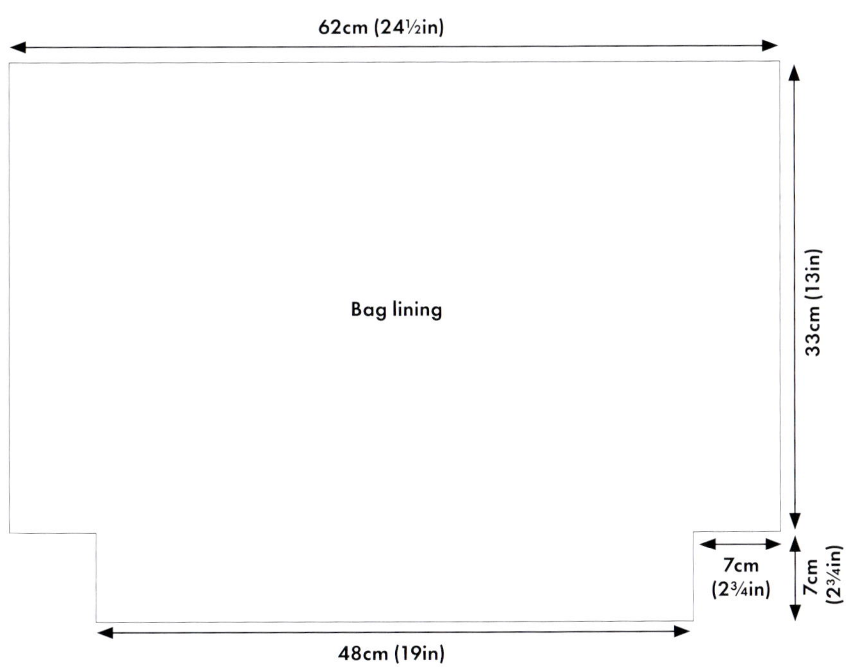

Prepare the outer raffia tote bag

14 The bag piece with your finished embroidery may have indentations from the hoop. You can smooth these out with an iron. To do this, place a piece of scrap fabric or an old bed sheet over your embroidery to protect it. Gently press the embroidery with a warm iron over the protective layer.

Important: avoid ironing directly on synthetic raffia as it will melt.

15 Using fabric scissors, carefully cut around both stitched tote bag shapes, staying just outside the stitching line.

16 Attach the straps:

a Position the straps: place one strap on the top edge of each tote bag piece, aligning the strap edges with the top edge of the fabric.

b Measure and pin: position each end of the strap 6cm (2½in) away from the centre. Pin the straps securely into place.

c Stitch: sew along the edges of the straps to secure them to the tote bag pieces.

17 Sew the sides:

a Place the front and back tote bag pieces, right sides together.

b Pin the left, right, and bottom edges together.

c Sew the pinned edges using a 3.5 stitch length and a 1.5cm (½in) seam allowance. Iron open each seam after you sew it.

18 Create the corners:

a Open one of the bottom corners of the bag.

b Bring the side and bottom seams together, ensuring they align and pin in place.

c Sew along the edge of the corner, using a 1.5cm (½in) seam.

d Repeat the same process for the second corner.

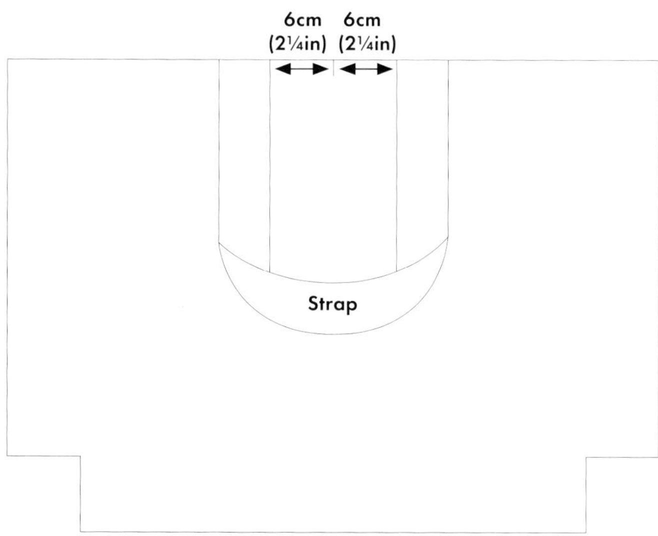

Prepare the tote bag lining

19 Using fabric scissors, carefully cut around both stitched rectangular facing shapes, staying just outside the stitching line.

20 Right sides together, position a facing piece with the top of the lining piece and pin in place. Sew together.

21 Press open the facing and lining seam and then press the seam towards the facing.

22 Stitch along the edge of the facing, 5mm (¼in) from the edge, to hold the seam in place.

23 Repeat steps 21–23 for the second lining piece.

24 Sew the sides:

a Place the front and back lining tote bag pieces, right sides together, ensuring that the facing seams align.

b Pin the left, right, and bottom edges together.

c Sew the left and right pinned edges using a 3.5 stitch length and a 1.5cm (½in) seam allowance. Iron open each seam as you sew.

d For the bottom, sew just 4cm (1½in) on each end with a 1.5cm (½in) seam allowance, leaving a gap in the middle.

25 Create the corners:

a Open one of the bottom corners of the bag.

b Bring the side and bottom seams together, ensuring they align and pin in place.

c Sew along the edge of the corner, using a 1.5cm (½in) seam allowance.

d Repeat the same process for the second corner.

Assemble the tote bag

26 Turn the outer raffia tote bag to the right side so the palm tree embroidery is visible.

27 Place the outer bag inside the lining, aligning the right sides together, and pin or clip the top edges together, matching the side seams.

28 Sew along the top edge using a 3.5 stitch length and a 1.5cm (½in) seam allowance.

29 Pull the outer bag out from the bottom of the lining, where you left a gap.

30 Iron the sewn seam flat and then press it towards the lining facing. Stitch along the edge of the facing, 5mm (¼in) from the edge, to secure the seam.

31 Turn the bag open so the right side of the outer bag is visible, and the lining is inside.

32 Pull out the bottom of the lining where the gap is. Press the gap in the lining closed neatly with an iron. Top stitch along the bottom of the lining.

33 Finally, push the lining inside the bag and give the bag a final press so that it sits neatly.

Finish the seams (optional)

34 To prevent fraying and enhance durability, carefully apply a thin layer of clear-drying glue into the raffia seams of the tote bag with a small paintbrush.

35 Allow the glue to dry completely for 24 hours.

SUNGLASSES SLEEVE

Keep your glasses safe from scratches with this raffia sunglasses sleeve. This project uses the back stitch to create a colourful and eye-catching design inspired by the vibrant Madras fabric, used by many Caribbean countries for their national dress.

FINISHED SIZE

- 10 x 18cm (4 x 7in)

MATERIALS

- 30 x 30cm (12 x 12in) piece of raffia fabric
- 30 x 30cm (12 x 12in) piece of fusible stretch interfacing
- 15 x 10cm (6 x 4in) piece of fusible woven interfacing
- 30 x 30cm (12 x 12in) piece of cotton fabric for lining
- Sewing machine thread in cream
- Embroidery thread in orange
- Fabric glue
- PVA glue
- Snap fastener (6mm/½in)
- Template from page 110

RAFFIA RIBBON COLOURS

- Light blue, orange, yellow

EQUIPMENT

- 20cm (7¾in) quilting hoop
- Carbon paper
- Toothed tracing wheel
- Fine-tip permanent marker, brown
- Chenille needle
- Sewing needle
- Fabric scissors
- Paper scissors
- Embroidery scissors
- Dressmakers' pins
- Sewing clips
- Sewing machine
- Iron
- Glue brush

Prepare the raffia

1 Prepare the raffia fabric using the method on page 20.

Transfer the glasses sleeve template

2 Measure and draw two 12 x 20cm (4¾ x 7¾in) rectangles onto the prepared raffia fabric using a ruler and fine-tip marker pen. This size includes a 1cm (¼in) seam allowance on all sides. You will have two glasses sleeve shapes drawn beside each other.

3 Set your sewing machine to the longest stitch length. Sew a line around the entire perimeter of the shapes you just marked. Make sure the stitches stay within the drawn line. This sewn line will prevent the raffia from fraying when you cut it out later.

4 Use template from page 110 and carefully position it in the centre of one of the glasses sleeve template shapes.

5 Transfer the design to the raffia using carbon paper and a tracing wheel. Refer to page 22 for detailed instructions on how to do this.

6 Repeat steps 4 and 5 to create a second glasses sleeve template.

Embroidery

7 Place your raffia with the transferred design in the embroidery hoop. Try to fit both rectangle template shapes in the hoop. If both do not fit, you can work section by section, moving the embroidery hoop as needed.

8 Follow the lines of the design with back stitches (see page 29). Start with the vertical lines and then follow with the horizontal lines. Use the illustration opposite as a guide for colours.

9 Do not tie knots at the beginning or end of the stitches lines to reduce bulk.

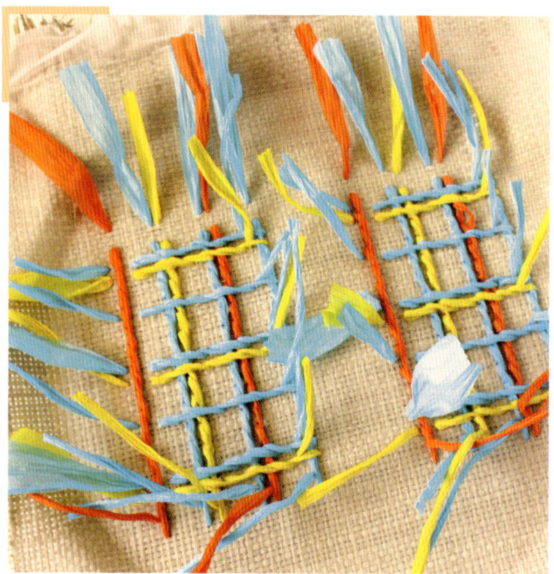

10 Once finished with the embroidery, remove the hoop.

11 Using PVA glue, stick down the loose ends at the beginning and end of the stitches, trimming with scissors as needed, as shown on page 25. Leave to dry fully for at least an hour.

Prepare the lining

12 Prepare your lining fabric by ironing it to smooth wrinkles and then fold it in half, aligning the selvedge edges.

13 Measure and draw two 11 x 20cm (4¼ x 7¾in) rectangles onto the lining fabric using a ruler and tailors' chalk.

14 Carefully cut around the rectangles, going through both layers, to create two identical lining pieces.

15 Using tailor's chalk, mark the position for the snap fasteners at the centre of a short edge of each lining piece, 1.5cm (½in) in from the edge. Mark each spot with a small dot. This will be the top edge.

16 Cut out two pieces of lining interfacing, each measuring 2.5 x 11cm (1 x 4½in).

17 Iron one lining interfacing piece to the top edge of each lining piece on the wrong side, following the manufacturer's instructions.

Sew on the snap fasteners

18 Separate the two parts of the snap fasteners.

19 Thread a sewing needle and tie a knot at the end of the thread. Use a sewing needle that will fit through the holes of the snap fastener pieces.

20 Place one side of the snap at the top centre of one of the lining pieces (where you marked with tailors' chalk in step 15).

21 Holding the snap in place with your non-dominant hand, bring the needle up from the wrong side of the fabric through one of the holes.

22 Bring the needle over the edge of the snap and push it down through the fabric, then pull the needle back up through the same hole. Repeat this between three and five times.

23 Sew through each hole in the same way to secure the snap. Then turn to the wrong side and tie a knot.

24 Repeat steps 20–23 on the other lining piece with the other side of the snap.

Sew the lining

25 Place the front and back lining pieces right sides together, then pin the left, right and bottom edges together.

26 Sew the pinned edges using a 3.5 stitch length and a 1cm (½in) seam allowance.

27 Finger-press and or iron the seams open where possible.

28 Fold over the top of the lining by 1cm (½in) towards the wrong side and press with an iron.

Prepare the outer glasses sleeve

29 The raffia piece with your finished embroidery on may have indentations from the hoop. You can smooth these out with an iron. To do this, place a piece of scrap fabric or an old bed sheet over your embroidery to protect it. Gently press the embroidery with a warm iron over the protective layer.

Important: avoid ironing directly on synthetic raffia as it will melt.

30 Using fabric scissors, carefully cut around both stitched pouch shapes, staying just outside the drawn line and making sure not to cut through stitches.

31 Sew the sides:

a Place the front and back sleeve pieces, right sides together.

b Pin/clip the left, right and bottom edges together.

c Sew the pinned edges using a 3.5 stitch length and a 1cm (½in) seam allowance.

d Carefully finger-press the seams open

32 Turn the sleeve right side out:

a Starting from the bottom of the sleeve, push through the corners and bottom.

b Carefully pull through the bottom to turn the sleeve right side out. This part can be tricky, so take your time with it.

c Once turned through, flatten the seams with your hands or carefully iron it flatter by placing a piece of scrap fabric or an old bed sheet over your embroidery to protect it.

33 Fold 1cm (½in) at the top of the sleeve towards the wrong side and press with an iron, keeping the side seam allowances open.

32

33

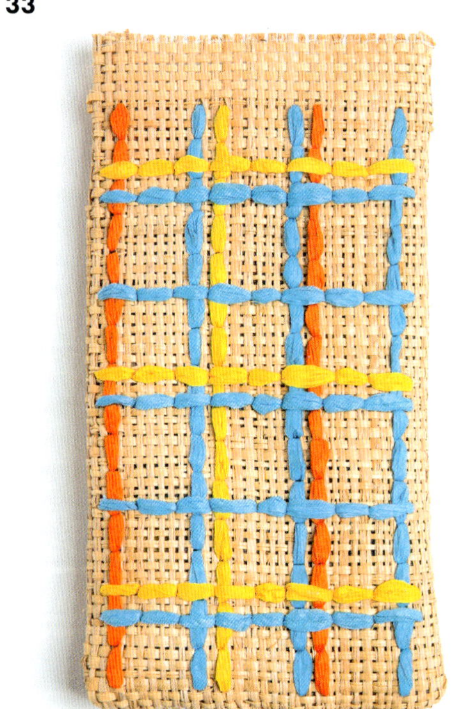

Assemble the glasses sleeve

34 Place the lining inside the raffia sleeve and push it down until the folded tops line up. Be sure to match the side seams.

35 Using fabric clips, clip the lining and the raffia sleeve together in place at the top.

36 Cut about an arm's length of embroidery thread, thread it through the chenille needle and tie a knot at the end.

37 Sew the top of the glasses case together to attach the lining to the outer raffia piece using a blanket stitch (see page 31) starting by sewing just through the raffia layer to hide the knot.

FRAMED ART

Brighten up your space with this uplifting raffia embroidery framed art. Use the fill stitch to embroider the phrase 'Don't Worry About a Thing' and create a beautiful piece of wall art.

FINISHED SIZE

- 35 x 38cm (13¾ x 15in), including fringe

MATERIALS

- 40 x 50cm (15¾ x 19¼in) piece of raffia fabric
- 40 x 50cm (15¾ x 19¼in) piece of fusible stretch interfacing
- Sewing machine thread in cream
- Picture frame to fit 40 x 50cm (15¾ x 19¼in)
- 40 x 50cm (15¾ x 19¼in) piece of 300gsm card
- PVA glue
- Double-sided tape
- Templates from pages 124–125

RAFFIA RIBBON COLOURS

- Green, orange, pink, yellow

EQUIPMENT

- 30cm (12in) quilting hoop
- Carbon paper
- Toothed tracing wheel
- Fine-tip permanent marker, brown
- Chenille needle
- Fabric scissors
- Paper scissors
- Embroidery scissors
- Dressmakers' pins
- Sewing machine
- Iron
- Glue brush

DON'T
WORRY
ABOUT A
THING

Prepare the raffia

1 Prepare the raffia fabric using the method on page 20.

Transfer the embroidery template

2 On a piece of paper draw a 25 x 27.5cm (9¾ x 10¾in) rectangle and cut it out. Secure this rectangle firmly in place with pins at the centre of your prepared raffia fabric at each of the four corners, leaving around 6cm (2½in) of raffia fabric on all sides for the fringe that will be added later.

3 Set your sewing machine to a stitch length of 3.5. Sew a line around the entire perimeter of the paper rectangle. Make sure the stitches don't go through the paper. This sewn line will help create the fringe around your embroidery later.

4 Remove the paper rectangle. Using the templates from pages 124–125, transfer the design to the raffia using a tracing wheel and carbon paper. Refer to page 22 for detailed instructions on how to do this.

Embroidery

5 Place your raffia with the transferred design in the embroidery hoop. Try to fit the whole design in the hoop otherwise, you can work section by section, moving the embroidery hoop as needed.

6 Fill in the letters with a raffia fill stitch (see page 30) following the colours and arrows in the illustration below.

Note: do not knot your raffia at the beginning or end of stitches. Leave the ends loose on the back of your work.

Finish the back of your embroidery

7 Once you've finished the embroidery, remove the raffia fabric from the embroidery hoop.

8 Turn your work over to the back. Trim the loose raffia ribbon ends leaving 1–2cm (½–¾in).

9 Use PVA glue to secure these ends to the back of the raffia design, as shown on page 27. Allow the glue to dry completely.

Create the fringe

10 From one corner of the raffia, peel away the interfacing up to the stitch lines.

11 With embroidery scissors (for extra precision!), trim off the peeled-away interfacing. Be super cautious not to snip through your stitching lines as this holds the fringe and prevents further fraying.

12 Gently pull on the vertical and horizontal strands of raffia where you just removed the interfacing until you reach the stitch line to create the fringe.

13 Trim the fringe down until each side of the fringe is about 4cm (1½in) so that it can fit in the frame.

Frame the embroidery

14 Take your 40 x 50cm (15¾ x 19½in) piece of card and lay your raffia embroidery centrally over the top.

15 Use a small piece of double-sided tape on each corner to attach the raffia embroidery to the card. This will prevent it from slipping down in the frame.

16 Place the card with the embroidery attached in your frame and close the back, following the instructions of your frame.

DENIM JACKET

Give your denim jacket a tropical makeover with this simple and fun raffia embroidery project. Use raffia fill stitch and stem stitch to create a vibrant pineapple design and transform your old jacket into a stylish summer piece.

FINISHED SIZE

- Depends on your jacket; mine measures 34 x 34cm (13½ x 13½in), including fringe

MATERIALS

- Denim jacket
- Raffia fabric: size depends on your denim jacket
- Fusible stretch interfacing: size depends on your denim jacket
- Sewing machine thread in cream
- Pattern paper or plain paper
- Templates from pages 126–127

RAFFIA RIBBON COLOURS

- Dark green, light green, orange, yellow

EQUIPMENT

- 30cm (12in) quilting hoop
- Carbon paper
- Toothed tracing wheel
- Fine-tip permanent marker, brown
- Chenille needle
- Fabric scissors
- Paper scissors
- Embroidery scissors
- Dressmakers' pins
- Sewing machine
- Iron
- Pencil
- Ruler
- Measuring tape

Measure your denim jacket

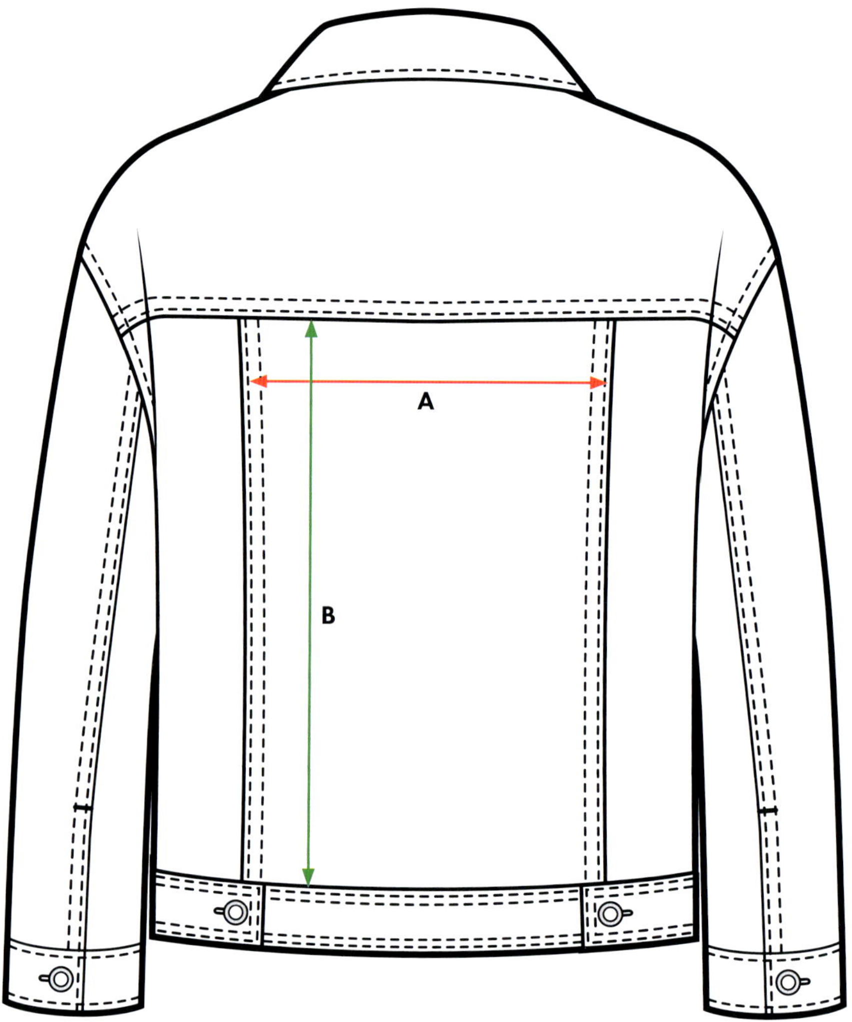

1 Before you get started, you need to work out the size that your raffia panel needs to be based on the denim jacket you will be using. To do this, measure the width between the two back seams (A) and the length from the yoke seam to the waistband seam (B).

Create your pattern

2 Draw a rectangle on pattern paper or plain paper using your denim jacket measurements. The dimensions for the rectangle are are:

width + 2cm (A + 2cm) x length (B)
(¾in) (¾in)

The pineapple embroidery design will be placed inside this rectangle.

3 Add 4cm (1½in) to the top and bottom for the hem, then 5cm (2in) to the left and right for the fringe.

4 Carefully cut out around the outer edges of your rectangle pattern.

5 You may need to resize the pineapple template from pages 126–127 to fit inside the rectangle, depending on the size of your denim jacket. If you need to resize it, use a photocopier to reduce or enlarge the pineapple template, then print it out.

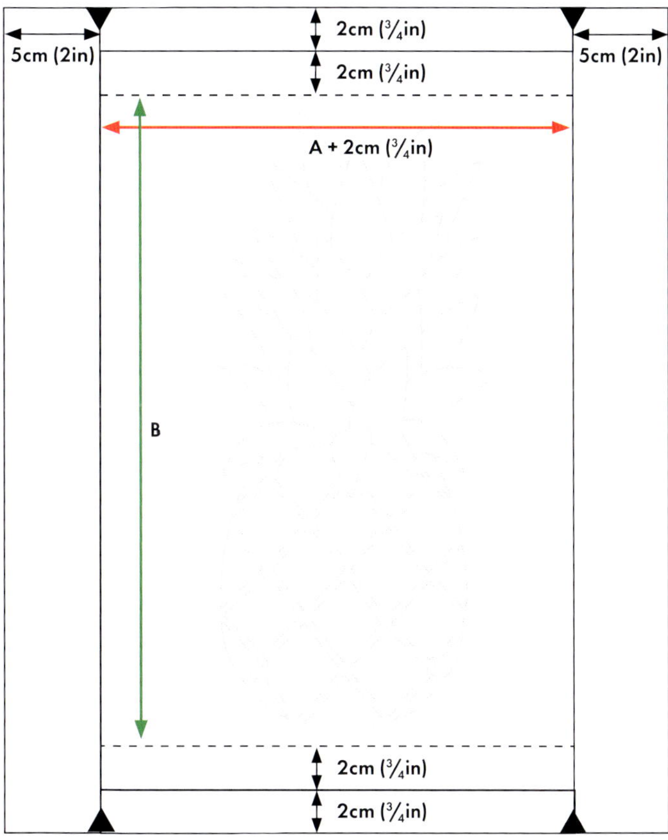

Prepare the raffia

6 Prepare the raffia fabric using the method on (page 20).

Transfer your pattern to raffia

7 Place the rectangular pattern you created on your prepared raffia fabric. Secure it firmly in place with pins at each of the four corners.

8 Using a fine-tip marker pen, draw around your rectangle pattern onto the raffia fabric. Remember to mark the 5cm (2in) measurements from each corner on both the top and bottom lines with a small line (these correspond to the black triangles in the diagram). Remove the paper pattern from the raffia once you've drawn around it.

9 Set your sewing machine to the longest stitch length. Sew a line around the entire perimeter of the rectangle shape you just marked. Make sure the stitches stay within the drawn line. This sewn line will prevent the raffia from fraying when you cut it out later.

10 Now, switch your sewing machine to a medium stitch length. Using this setting, sew two straight vertical lines from the top edge of your rectangle down to the bottom, following the marks you made for the black triangles on the template. These stitched lines will hold the raffia strands in place for the fringe you'll create later.

Transfer the pineapple template

11 Take your resized pineapple template and carefully position it in the centre on the raffia (see diagram on page 105). Secure it with pins to keep it in place.

12 Transfer the design to the raffia using carbon paper and a tracing wheel. Refer to the techniques section (page 30) for detailed instructions on how to do this.

Embroidery

13 Place your raffia with the transferred design in the embroidery hoop. Try to fit as much of the design in the hoop as possible, but don't worry you can move the hoop around as you work.

14 Fill in the leaves and yellow pineapple diamond shapes with raffia fill stitch (see page 30) following the colours and direction in the photos.

15 Embroider stem stitch (see page 32) in orange between the yellow diamond shapes.

Prepare your raffia panel

16 Your finished embroidery may have indentations from the hoop. You can smooth these out with an iron. To do this, place a piece of scrap fabric or an old bedsheet over your embroidery to protect it. Gently press the embroidery with a warm iron over the protective layer.

Important: avoid ironing directly on synthetic raffia as it will melt.

17 Grab your fabric scissors. Carefully cut along the rectangular shape you previously stitched, staying just outside the stitching line to avoid cutting through stitches.

18 To prevent fraying, finish the edges of the raffia at the top and bottom. If you have an overlocker, use this to stitch along these two sides. Otherwise, use a zigzag stitch on your sewing machine.

Remove the interfacing and create the fringe

19 Focus on the right and left sides of the rectangle of raffia fabric. Here, snip away the stitches that hold these sides closed. Plus, cut away the 5cm (2in) of overlocked or zigzag stitches from the corners at the top and bottom.

20 Next comes the fun part – creating the fringe! Locate the fusible stretch interfacing from the right and left sides. Peel it away carefully, stopping at the stitch lines. Don't remove any interfacing beyond the stitching.

21 With embroidery scissors (for extra precision!), trim off the peeled-away interfacing. Be super cautious not to snip through your stitching lines as this holds the fringe and prevents further fraying.

22 Gently pull on a single vertical strand of raffia where you just removed the interfacing. This will start the unravelling process. Keep pulling out vertical raffia strands until you reach the stitch line. Repeat this process on both sides.

Hemming

23 Time to create a clean finish! Use your iron to fold and press the top and bottom edges up 2cm (¾in). With your sewing machine, sew along to secure the hem.

Attach raffia panel to denim jacket

24 Lay the denim jacket open on a flat surface right side up. Place your finished raffia panel in the centre of the back. Line up the top hem with the yoke seam at the top, and the bottom hem with the waistband seam at the bottom.

25 One you have the panel in the right position, secure it into place with a few pins.

26 Sew around the perimeter of the panel (not over the fringe) to secure the panel onto the denim jacket.

TEMPLATES

All templates are printed at 100% scale. See page 22 for how to transfer the templates to raffia fabric.

The templates for some of the larger projects will need to be traced or photocopied onto plain paper and then assembled into the correct formation before transferring to your fabric. Please refer to the positioning diagrams supplied in these instances (for example the Pillow Cover templates on page 114–119).

The charts are also available to download from the Bookmarked Hub: www.bookmarkedhub.com

Search for this book by title or ISBN: the files can be found under 'Book Extras'.

Sunglasses Sleeve, page 86

Monstera Leaf Hoop Art,
page 40
Banana Decoration,
page 60

Parrot Wall Hanging, page 52

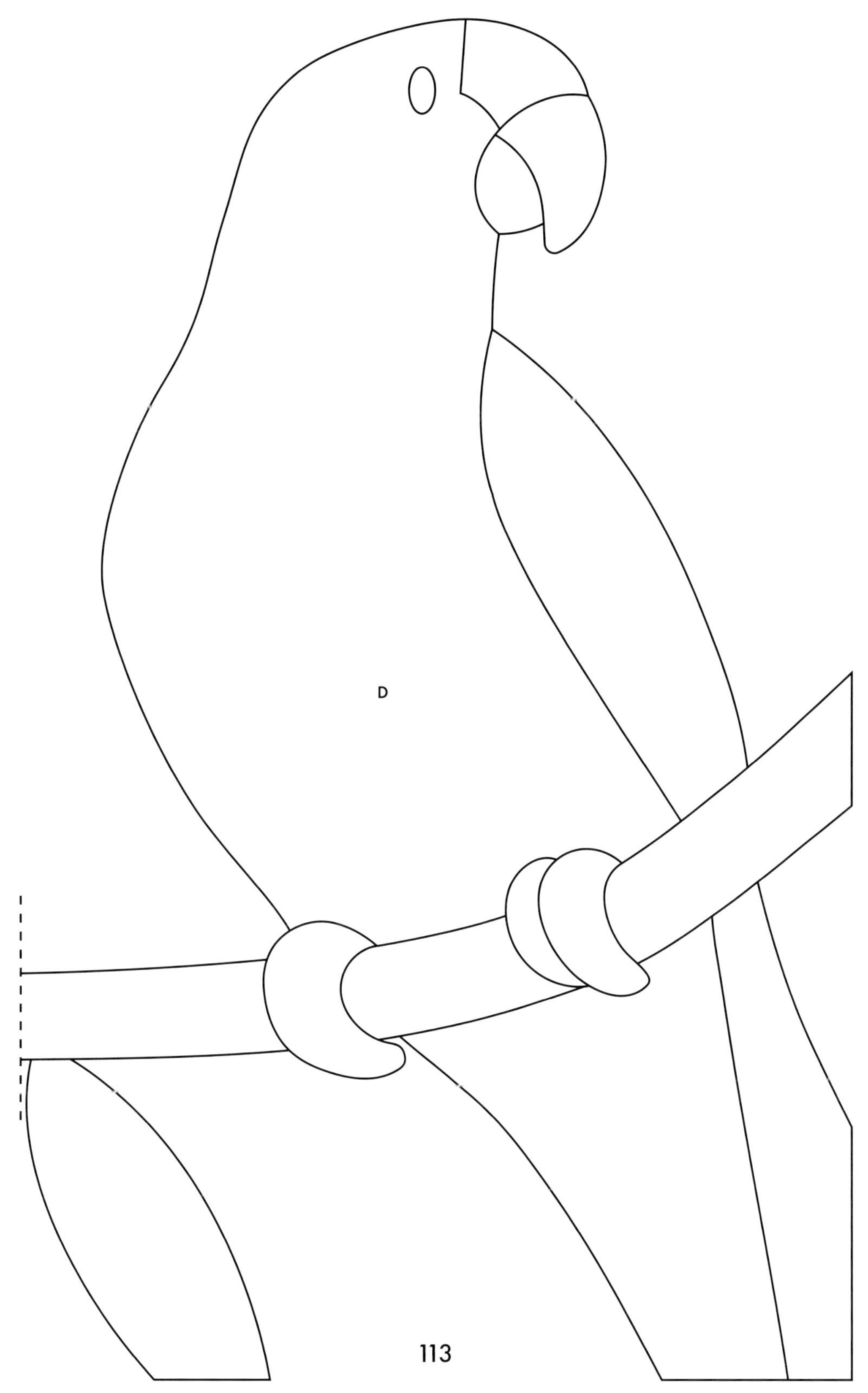
D

Pillow Cover, page 66

A
B
C
TAKE IT
EASY
D
D
F
A
E
E

D
C

Pillow Cover, page 66

F

TAK
E IT

Pillow Cover, page 66

Note: arrange the letter templates on your fabric to form the words shown in colour on page 115.

Hibiscus Zipped Pouch, page 72

Tote Bag, page 78

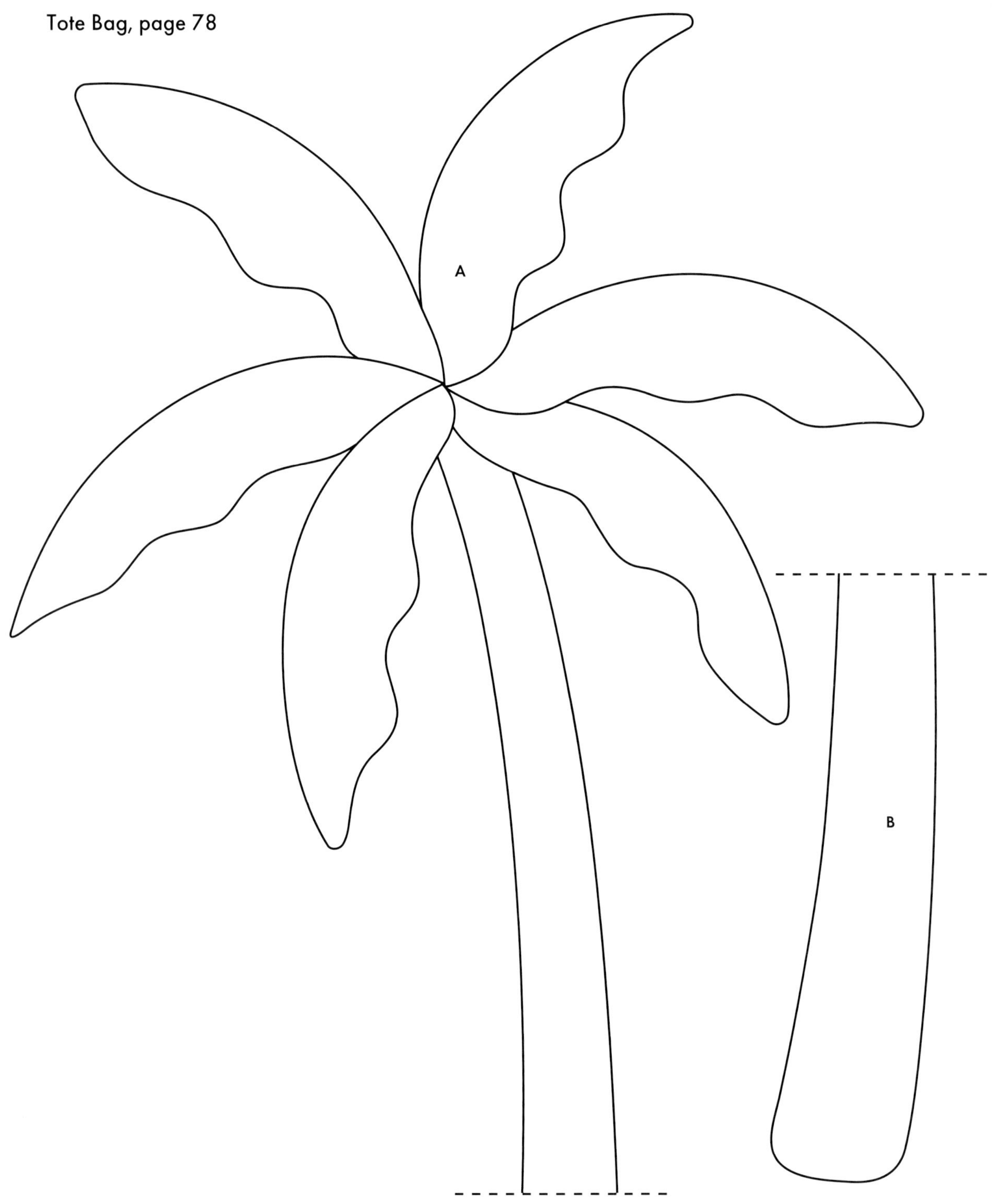

C
A
C
B

Framed Art, page 96

Note: arrange the letter templates on your fabric to form the words shown in colour below.

ABOU
T A
THING

Denim Jacket, page 102

B
A
B

First published in 2026

Search Press Limited
Wellwood, North Farm Road,
Tunbridge Wells, Kent TN2 3DR

1 2 3 4 5 6 7 8 9 10

ISBN: 978-1-80092-303-4
ebook ISBN: 978-1-80093-291-3

Editor: Carrie Baker
Managing Editor: Becky Robbins
Head of Design: Marrianne Miall
Publishing Director: Samantha Warrington

Bookmarked Hub
Extra copies of the templates are available to download free from the Bookmarked Hub. Search for this book by title or ISBN: the files can be found under 'Book Extras'. Membership of the Bookmarked online community is free: www.bookmarkedhub.com

Publishers' notes
Metric measurements are used in this book; the imperial conversions are rounded to the nearest ¼in. Always use either metric or imperial measurements, not a combination of both.

The Publishers and author can accept no responsibility for any consequences arising from the information, advice or instructions given in this publication.

For errata, please visit our website (www.searchpress.com) or the Bookmarked Hub (www.bookmarkedhub.com).

GPSR information can be found at www.searchpress.com

Printed in China, RRD102025